LEARN TO SHARE THE GOOD NEWS

*Evangelism and
the Local Church*

S<small>TEPHEN</small> M<small>C</small>Q<small>UOID</small>

First published 2019 by Partnership (UK) Ltd and OPAL Trust

Partnership (UK) Ltd, Abbey Court, Cove, Tiverton EX16 7RT, UK

23 22 21 20 19 / 5 4 3 2 1

British Library Cataloguing in Publication Data

A catalogue record for this book is available from the British Library

ISBN 978-0-9570177-7-1

Typeset and cover design by projectluz.com
Printed and bound in Great Britain
for Partnership (UK) Ltd and OPAL Trust
by Bell & Bain, Glasgow

Series Preface

While this book is a revision of an earlier book, published by Partnership in 2002,[1] it now forms part of a series being published jointly by OPAL Trust[2] and Partnership[3] with the collaboration of GLO Europe[4] and Tilsley College[5]. The titles which are part of this *Learning to …* series so far are:

> David Clarkson and Stephen McQuoid, *Learning to Lead: Next Generation*, OPAL Trust, 2013
>
> Stephen McQuoid, *Learning to Share the Good News: Evangelism and the Local Church*, OPAL Trust & Partnership, 2019
>
> Jeremy McQuoid and Stephen McQuoid, *Learning to Preach*, OPAL Trust & Partnership, forthcoming 2019.

---

1 Under the title of *Sharing the Good News in C21: Evangelism in a local church context*.

2 **OPAL [Overseas Publishing and Literature] Trust** provides literature for the Majority World. It provides affordable Bibles and other good Christian literature to missionaries and national workers alike, in many countries worldwide, and has permanent book depots in Zambia and the USA, as well as in the UK.

3 **Partnership** has existed for a number of decades specifically to encourage, strengthen, and support local independent evangelical churches which are committed to the biblical gospel and to team leadership and every member ministry. One way in which it does this is through publications (including the thrice-yearly *Partnership Perspectives*) aimed particularly to help church leaders and other volunteer workers. It is in close contact with some 350 churches in the UK.

4 **GLO Europe** is a Christian mission organization dedicated to bringing the good news of Jesus to a world that is lost. Its vision is to establish church planting teams throughout Europe and to support them and local churches through short-term mission trips. It is also committed to training and equipping Christians for mission and ministry so that they can share God and their faith effectively.

5 **Tilsley College** is the training arm of GLO Europe and is based at Motherwell in Scotland. It offers a range of one-, two-, and three-year accredited residential courses at very economical fee-rates (all including significant, on-the-job placement experience), part-time study through open access to the College's regular teaching, evening class study in local areas (Joshua Training), and online study.

These titles are an example of collaboration between bodies which serve a large group of independent local churches which are found in the UK and in possibly as many as 150 or more countries across the world.

The purpose of the series is to provide material of help to church leaders, and others who are active in church life and work, in local churches which, because they are committed to team leadership and every-member ministry, have many unpaid church leaders and other volunteers who are vital to the life of their churches. Many of these church workers have had little time and opportunity for formal training for their responsibilities: they are keen students of Scripture, have active devotional lives, and often much experience in the Christian service which they undertake. But, for the most part, as has been said of the armies of the American Civil War, they have learned 'to march by marching and to shoot by shooting'. Such leaders and workers are essential to the life and work of the church, and it is evidently impossible and in principle gravely limiting for Christian ministry to be carried out exclusively by trained, paid workers. But, very often, volunteer workers are only too conscious that they could do better if they had some 'continuous professional development' (CPD) for their tasks. It is the purpose of this series to provide relevant and helpful material which can be used in this way. For some topics in the series, the material will simply be print; while for others there will be related audio-visual material supplementing the print and a related training course which is accessible online (as is the case with *Learning to Lead*—see https://glo-europe.org/tilsley/learningtolead.html for more details).

While the aim of this series is to help voluntary Christian workers, we have no doubt that those who have had the privilege of formal training for Christian work, can profit from the books in this series, if only by way of 'brush-up' and CPD for themselves!

The books in this series are not produced for profit by commercial entities, nor do writers and editors normally receive remuneration for their work. Any surpluses on sales will be used to finance further such publications and to subsidize the distribution of books in the Majority World, so that church leaders and others can benefit from them when otherwise they would not be able to do so.

Contents

Preface

When I *wrote Sharing the Good News in C21: Evangelism in a local church context* back in 2002, I began by admitting that I am no expert when it comes to doing evangelism, even though I teach it. I love sharing my faith with people, and I have had the incredible joy of leading some to personal faith in Jesus Christ. However, I wish I were more creative and inventive, I wish I had more courage, and I certainly wish that I had led more people into faith, as it is the single most important thing in life. This substantially enlarged and updated book is not written because I am an expert, but simply because I have a passion for evangelism.

Evangelism has never been easy, but arguably it is getting more difficult all the time. In general, people in Western society today are more sceptical about Christianity, are more entrenched in their worldviews, and have more reasons for not believing than at any other time. The gospel has to compete in a world crowded with other ideas and, even though we know it to be true and the opposing views to be false, it still doesn't make the job of evangelism any easier.

I have enlarged my earlier book because I am anxious that we, in all our churches, should get a renewed vision to share the gospel with a dying world and that we should use all means possible to ensure the job gets done. Churches do not find evangelism convenient or smooth. Often, they become discouraged and feel like giving up. They need to be reminded that Jesus commanded us to take the gospel to the world. This was God's plan for church growth. And church leaderships tend to focus almost exclusively on existing believers in their care, particularly on teaching and pastoral care. This is good in itself, of course, but they often neglect evangelism and frequently don't have among them people with the gift of the evangelist, and don't encourage those in their congregations who have it.

Only history will show the extent to which we have been obedient, as our survival depends on the extent to which we obey Christ's command in the Great Commission. But it is not enough merely to have the desire to evangelise; in a changing world, we need to evangelise in a way that will be relevant to our society.

My prayer is, first, that, as people read this book, they will be challenged to become more active in evangelism. Second, I pray that those who read will learn something that will help them relate the gospel more ably to their society. I still feel like an amateur when it comes to doing evangelism. Perhaps this will be the strength of this book. It is not a fail-safe guide to evangelism, but it is written by someone very ordinary who loves to talk about Jesus. If the ideas here have helped someone as deficient as I am, they will help you also.

As ever, I am indebted to so many people in the production of this book. I begin with my wife, Debbie, and my three children, Karis, Taylor and Jamie, who put up with me spending long evenings on my laptop rather than doing 'fun stuff' with them. Thanks also to Allison Hill, my assistant, who works hard to release me to do this kind of work, and to Simon Marshall, his predecessor, Mark Davies, and the staff at Tilsley College who still allow me to teach and develop this material. Also I constantly owe a debt of thanks to all of my Gospel Literature Outreach (GLO) colleagues in the UK and across Europe who continually inspire me by their commitment to the gospel. I would also like to offer a special thanks to a dear friend, Dr. Neil Summerton. He encouraged me to revise my earlier book, but more than that, he is a man who loves God, believes deeply in the power of the gospel, has a profound commitment to the church, and embodies the kind of wisdom, spirituality, kindness and self-sacrifice that I would love to aspire to. He has sub-edited and commented on this book to remove any blemishes that he spotted, and this is just one of the many tasks he does for the kingdom, which many will never be aware of.

About the Author

Stephen McQuoid grew up in Ethiopia where his parents were missionaries. He then lived in Ireland, where he qualified as a nurse before going on to study theology and enter full-time Christian ministry. He holds Masters and Doctoral degrees and has written more than a dozen books. Stephen is General Director of Gospel Literature Outreach, a missionary organisation based in Motherwell, Scotland. He is married to Debbie, and they, along with their three children, fellowship at Liberty Community Church, Belshill, where they are both on the Leadership Team.

CHAPTER 1

Four Stories in the Big Story

The acculturated Muslim

It was a long hot summer day in Strasbourg. I was in the famous French city attending the International Brethren Conference in Mission, a quadrennial event that brings church leaders together from all over the world to talk about issues such as evangelism, culture and the state of our churches. My brief at the conference was to do a seminar on the so-called 'New Atheists' and then preach at the closing plenary session.

I love events like that, not just because of the stimulating sessions that are on offer, but also because of the remarkable people you meet. Men and women who courageously lead their churches in a variety of challenging situations. There were, however, three issues that occurred to me on that particular day. Number one, the chairs were uncomfortable; two, the conference centre had no air-conditioning, which on such a sunny day was a struggle; and, three, I was so desperate to see something of the city itself that I found it difficult to concentrate on what was happening at the conference.

My solution was to sneak away just before lunch and catch a tram to the historic centre of Strasbourg. The city was every bit as impressive as the tourist brochures had promised. The Ill River, which flows through Strasbourg, surrounds the historic old town on all sides, making it an island. Pride of place in this UNESCO world heritage site goes to the cathedral, which has towered over the city for the best part of 800 years, its single spire reaching 142 metres into the air, making it the sixth tallest church in the world.

Feeling peckish, I began to look for a restaurant in the vicinity of the cathedral that would fill my stomach but not completely empty my wallet. I found one that did neither, but in the busyness of the tourist season it was my only option. The particular one I chose was a bistro situated within a small square just around the corner from the cathedral. The tables were tightly packed together and I found myself on a small table right next to a distinguished looking woman in her late fifties. Once I had ordered my meal, I felt I should say 'hello' to her, not least because of the close proximity of our two tables. My introduction began a fascinating conversation.

It turned out that the woman was on a day trip from neighbouring Germany and was the wife of a Turkish diplomat. In beautiful English, she explained to me that, although she was a Turkish national, she had spent almost all of her life in Germany and saw herself as being European not Asian, as some Turks perceive themselves to be. She had travelled extensively throughout Europe and felt most at home in a Western cultural context. Three months prior to that meal, I had been in Istanbul for a weekend and told her about my visit. When she enquired about my reason for going to Turkey, I told her I was a Christian and that I wanted to visit other Christians who were there. I assumed correctly that she would be a Muslim and wondered just how she would react to my declaration of faith. To my surprise, she was pleased to meet a Christian and wanted to discuss our respective faiths in more detail.

Our conversation went back and forward for a while. I told her about the importance of Jesus and his bodily resurrection, and how someone can become a Christian and be forgiven. She told me that Islam is all about submission to the will of Allah and that he blesses those who are obedient and pure. She then asked me about Christian attitudes to Islam and made a rather predictable reference to the Crusades. I explained to her that the Crusades did not in any way represent Jesus, who told us to love our enemies. She accepted this, told me that she had a great respect for Christians, and then apologised about the three Christian martyrs who had been killed in Turkey some months earlier.

The conversation continued for some time and it occurred to me that this was a woman who was very much part of the Europe I live in, someone who shared my love of freedom and democracy, someone who believed as I do in religious liberty, but someone who was a committed Muslim. She was no extremist; rather she was a reasonable and highly articulate exponent of Islam. She was also, because of what she believed, someone who rejected the gospel, believing it to be false. This rejection was not aggressive, violent or hostile, but it was a rejection of the Christian faith. She did not believe that Jesus was the Son of God or the Saviour of the world. She was a modern and cultured European woman whose religious worldview was the opposite of what I as a Christian was committed to. I still pray for her salvation, but recognise that it will take a work of the Holy Spirit to convict her of her need of Christ.

The modern Danes

I remember another very different conversation that I had with a young couple on the streets of Copenhagen. I was leading a team organised by Gospel Literature Outreach and on that particular evening we were conducting an open-air meeting on one of the busy pedestrianized streets of the city.

Our team was very good and highly motivated. They sang well and were able to perform some excellent street theatre. We ran several short presentations, finishing with a testimony or short evangelistic message, and then we would move into the crowd to engage people in conversation. It was at this point that I met this young couple whom I will call Jacob and Hilda, though I can't be sure that I remember their names correctly. They were typical of many young people in Denmark and throughout Europe. They were in their mid-twenties and, having graduated from university, found themselves in the big world of work. Both of them were bright and were hoping to climb rapidly up the career ladder. They had a concern for the damage that capitalism was doing to the world and a compassion for the poor, yet at the same time they enjoyed all the benefits that their generous pay packets brought them and even took it for granted that they would live lives of comfort and prosperity.

This young couple were unmarried and, indeed, had little intention of ever getting married, but they were living together and were clearly committed to their relationship. They were members of the state church, but, like most Danes, that fact meant nothing to them. Their biblical knowledge was virtually non-existent and they did not see Christianity as being any different from other world faiths. It was simply one of many religious options available to people in contemporary society. They had genuine doubts about the existence of God and felt that, if God did exist, he must be very hard to find. But they rejected atheism: the atheist was being too certain about something they could not be certain about. They were also interested in spirituality and held to several quasi-religious ideas that bordered on the superstitious. They believed that there were both good and evil spiritual forces operating in the world and that there was probably some form of existence beyond physical death.

I approached them for a conversation because, during one of our street theatre presentations, they were smiling and clearly enjoyed what they saw. I asked if they had understood what we were trying to communicate, and a good conversation began.

Coming from Northern Ireland, I have never had a problem about being direct with people. Within seconds I had launched into a description of the sinfulness of humankind and the fact that God is offended by our wayward behaviour. I then went on to talk about Jesus and his death on the cross, which, I insisted, was the only solution to the problem of sin. Next, I explained how the work of Jesus on the cross was able to remove all our sin, thus reconciling us with God, and I finished up stating how wonderful heaven was going to be and how much I was looking forward to getting there. It occurred to me that, up to that point, the conversation had been one-way traffic and I had not given them an opportunity to respond to anything that I was saying. However, I at least felt happy that I had said enough to persuade them of the truthfulness of my message. Unfortunately, I was greatly mistaken.

Jacob and Hilda were not put off by my approach to evangelism, but they were not convinced either. They were amused to find a relatively young person being so passionate about something as old-fashioned and quaint as religion, but they found my presentation fairly incomprehensible. To begin with, my description of the work of Christ and its effects was much too theologically advanced for them, because they had no recognition of their spiritual needs. To them sin, if it existed at all, included only such abominations as child abuse and murder. They certainly would not have seen their cohabitation as a sin and could not understand how a supposedly loving God would be so petty as to see their lives as being at fault.

Their belief about God was also very vague. They were aware that many Danes believe that science has removed the need to believe in God and are committed to both the theory of evolution and philosophical naturalism. Jacob and Hilda were sceptical about both positions, preferring to live with unanswered questions. Having been brought up in a thoroughly pluralist society, they were also of the view that every religion was equally true and valid, and that to disagree with this position was tantamount to bigotry. But there was another issue still. They were well off and lived in a country where the social services provided a network that would help them, were they to run into difficulties. In short, their lives were comfortable and this had led to a great spiritual complacency. My urgency seemed to have little impact on this.

Quite bizarrely, the heavens opened and heavy rain came down, soaking the three of us as we talked. Jacob and Hilda did not seem too perturbed that they were getting soaked, so I continued to witness to them. I shared my testimony and told them of the great joy I had being a Christian and having a personal relationship with the God of the universe. They were certainly interested in this and Jacob even declared, 'I am happy for you that you seem to have found answers to your life questions'. He was not being funny or sarcastic; I think he really meant it. But as the rain continued to pour down, I knew that what was needed was not only more time to share the gospel with this couple who were genuinely open, but also a different approach. The gospel is unchanging, but its presentation needs to dovetail with the understanding and cultural assumptions of those who hear.

The committed Catholic

A third conversation that comes to mind took place in a football stadium. I have a friend who is a keen supporter of Glasgow Rangers. He invited me to come with him for a game and, being a huge football fan, I took up the invitation with enthusiasm. As we sat in our seats waiting for the players to emerge from the tunnel, my friend Alan introduced me to a young university student who sat in the row behind. Alan is a committed Christian and had been witnessing to the young man Saturday by Saturday throughout the season. To get a conversation going, Alan asked the young guy, whose name was Gary, to tell me what he had done the night before. Gary responded with a slightly sheepish look on his face by telling me that the previous night he had been at Mass. This slightly surprised me, as most Rangers fans tend to be at least nominally Protestant, whereas fans of their great rivals, Celtic, tend to be Roman Catholic. Seeing a Catholic loudly cheering Rangers is an uncommon sight in the west of Scotland.

I quickly put Gary's mind at rest by telling him that I was a Christian. It was obvious to me that he had felt the pressure of living in a very secular society where religious faith was often scorned. I then asked him why he was a Catholic. I fully expected him simply to say that his parents were Catholic and that he just inherited his faith. As it happens, they were, but instead he replied that he was Catholic because he believed the message which the Catholic Church preached was true and that having a faith was important to him. He was interested in history and he realised that the Catholic Church had a long history which, he felt, gave it credibility. For him, it was the official voice of Christendom. He had great respect for evangelical Christians, but they were just an offshoot of the real Church. Gary is one of a declining number of people in Scotland and the UK at large who are committed to Catholicism. But while their numbers are declining, they remain significant, as do adherents of the Orthodox Church in all their varieties. These historic Churches hold to creeds and traditions that do not always align with Scripture. Whether it is the sacrifice of the Mass, confession to a priest or the veneration of Mary, issues arise that can distract worshippers from a simple faith in Christ and his death on the cross. Yet often, even in the face of biblical proclamation, adherents refuse to accept that simple faith, believing that the historic traditions of the Catholic or Orthodox Churches must be correct, as they have such an established history.

The convinced atheist

A final conversation took place on the streets of London during the 2012 Olympics. I was there once again with a GLO summer team, trying to proclaim the gospel to the many thousands of visitors who had come to the great event. On one of the days, I took the team to Ealing Broadway to work with a friend of mine who is an evangelist and street preacher. Our method was simple. We simply carried a small box to a busy part of the high street, near the train station, and took it in turns to stand up and preach to the bustling crowds that went by. After each sermon we would try and engage people in conversation.

One of our team members was a 16-year-old girl who was a very powerful and engaging preacher. I stood a few metres away to watch what went on. A man near me looked interested in what the girl had to say, but when she got to a point where she began talking about God's judgment, he began to shout out abusive comments at her. I quickly moved over to where he stood and asked him why he was being so rude. He replied, using very colourful language, that he was an atheist and that he hated religious people because they were all such hypocrites. I decided not to tackle the issue of his perception of religious people, but rather just told him that I did not have enough faith to be an atheist.

He was taken by surprise by my statement, as he assumed that atheists are the rational ones, whereas religious people are the ones who rely on faith. When he asked what I meant by that, I said that there must surely be a reason why the universe exists and that if you leave God out of the equation there is no credible explanation left; all you have left, if you are committed to atheism, is blind faith. This led to a lengthy discussion ranging from evolution and intelligent design right through to human morality and religious experience.

It became clear to me that this man, whose name was Charles, was a well-educated and thoughtful individual. He had read extensively and had a particular interest in the sciences. His thinking had been greatly influenced by noted atheists such as Richard Dawkins and the late Christopher Hitchens. Charles was actually much less hostile towards people of faith than first appeared. However, he believed that scientists held the intellectual high ground and that religion falls within the realm of belief, superstition and faith, whereas science is about truth and facts. This worldview would inevitably make evangelism very difficult, as anything I might say would be met with a deep-seated scepticism.

The implications for evangelism

These four conversations could have taken place in any British city, indeed any city in Europe. We live in a very complex culture where many worldviews and belief systems exist and where no two people think in the same way. We therefore need to give serious thought to the issue of evangelism and how we go about it. Before we do so, there are a few reflections that I think are worth noting.

First, evangelism is not just about what we say, but the work that the Holy Spirit does in the lives of those to whom we witness. We should never feel that the ultimate responsibility of reaching others is ours, or that we have 'blown it' if a conversation does not work out as we expected. The Holy Spirit is sovereign and we need the faith to believe that he can use our faltering words to convict people of their sin.

Second, although some people may struggle to understand the gospel when we explain it to them, it is nevertheless relevant and exactly what they need. Every time I share my faith with someone, I am forcefully reminded that this message is the only one that can change people's lives and the only hope of salvation. Any difficulties that I have had in sharing my faith have in no way discouraged me or left me feeling that I have nothing to offer people. On the contrary, with every difficult evangelistic experience I am more determined to try even harder next time, because I am ever more convinced of the truthfulness and necessity of the gospel.

Third, I am humbled as I think that God has entrusted the majestic gospel message to ordinary people like me. It is one of the great wonders of Christianity that when God makes his appeal to the world, he chooses to use ordinary men and women to do it. In this way, although the ultimate responsibility of reaching others is not ours, yet we still have a responsibility to do all we can, because God chooses to work through us.

Lastly, I am reminded that although the gospel message does not change and remains powerful in every generation, the way it is presented needs to change from place to place and era to era. We are not living in yesterday's world. We are living in today's world, a world that is constantly changing and reinventing itself, constantly presenting new challenges to the evangelist. We need to think long and hard about what to say and how to say it. That is what the rest of this book is about and I hope that you will find it useful.

Discussion Questions

1. Think of some of the conversations you have had in witnessing to non-Christians. What truths did you struggle to get across, and why?
2. When you are sharing your faith, what questions or objections do you find most difficult to deal with, and why?
3. Describe the worldview of your non-Christian contacts, and state in what ways you can make the gospel relevant to their situation.

CHAPTER 2

Living with the Footprints of History

When Jesus gave his Great Commission, commanding his followers to 'make disciples of all nations' (Mt. 28: 19), he was giving them the greatest challenge that they would ever face. Their role (and consequently ours) was to participate in the massive task of reaching every nation with the gospel, declaring to the world that salvation is freely available as a result of the death and resurrection of Jesus Christ. Even in those days with the world's population so much smaller than it is today, the scale of the task was mind-boggling. In today's world, with its seven billion people, its 6,909 languages, and its complex geopolitical landscape, the task seems even more daunting.

The scale of the task is such that many Christians and churches opt out of their responsibility, protesting that the job is just too hard. They might not do this openly, but they do it in practice by retreating behind their church walls rather than engaging with the hostile world outside. The assumption they make is that the world is just too sinful, too alien and too difficult to reach, so they do not even try. Or they are too comfortable in their church milieu and don't want it disturbed by others. This dereliction of duty pricks their consciences and so they organise completely ineffectual outreaches so that no one can accuse them of doing nothing. These outreaches might salve their consciences, but they do not reach people who are lost.

The Great Commission, however, is not some optional extra for those who are particularly enthused. We do not have the luxury of opting out and pretending that the responsibility for evangelism is not ours: Jesus said: 'You are the salt of the earth ... you are the light of the world' (Mt. 5: 13,14). It is not that we can be if we so desire; we are! The only salt and light that our world will have is the church, and that involves you and me. We are implicated in God's plan for world evangelism whether we like it or not. To ignore the Great Commission is to live in flagrant disobedience to Jesus Christ.

But the job is further complicated by Jesus' command that we should make disciples. It is not enough just to share the good news with people and help them take their first few steps of faith, as they make an initial commitment to Christ. If that is the extent of our ambition, then we risk losing many spiritual babies as they die of exposure in the hostile environment of our society. We are not to be mere spiritual scalp-hunters. The task of being a witness is not complete until the people we lead to Christ have become spiritually mature and capable of maintaining their own spiritual life. They need to become people who look like Jesus, think like Jesus, relate to others like Jesus and behave like Jesus, because this is what all disciples of Christ should aspire to become. The whole focus of our evangelism, therefore, needs to change. We need to think long-term, not short-term. Our aim must be to bring people to a point where they are mature Christians who can take responsibility for their own spiritual lives, rather than just settling for an instant decision. Only then are we complying with the terms of the Great Commission.

Where can we start, for the world is such a big place? The only place to start is where we are. Every Christian should have a world vision, but at the back of our minds should be an ever-present concern for lost men and women everywhere. Until God calls us to distant lands, we need to be active witnesses and evangelists in our own backyard. As individuals and churches, the expression of our concern for the world begins by reaching and discipling people within our own community. We each rub shoulders with people who do not have a relationship with Jesus. These people may be at our work, in our social life, or family members. It is with them that our obedience to the Great Commission begins.

Culture

When the first disciples heard the Great Commission, they recognized that they needed to communicate the gospel within a set cultural context. The message of the kingdom required a form of communication which would relate to the people of their generation. This is the very essence of evangelism: making spiritual truths understandable to unspiritual people. To do this, they needed to use the language of the devout Jew, the pious gentile, the Emperor-worshipper, those caught up in the Mystery Religions, and those who were the power-brokers of Rome. We can see this in practice in *Acts*, by contrasting the apostle Paul's presentations of the gospel in different synagogues (e.g., 13: 16–41), to the simple pagans of Lystra (14: 15–17), to the sophisticated citizens of Athens (17: 22–31), and before Roman procurators and kinglets (26: 2–29).

In much the same way, we need to communicate the gospel within our own cultural context. Today's culture is not only chronologically far removed from the culture of the Bible; it is also far removed in its assumptions and thought forms. The world has undergone not one but many cultural revolutions since biblical times, and we need therefore to grasp the essence of contemporary culture, so that our presentation is as relevant to our contemporaries as the message of those first disciples was to theirs.

The need to make our presentation relevant and up-to-date with current cultural trends is on-going. The rate of cultural change today is much more rapid than it was in the first century. Science, technology and the advent of the mass media have had an epochal impact on how Western society thinks and behaves. Whereas in past generations, it took months and even years for fads to catch on, in today's world it takes days, as new ideas and fashions become viral. During biblical times, if a citizen in Rome wanted to introduce a new product or idea to another city like Alexandria, it might take weeks for him to get there and share this new item with his target group. Today, the Internet will convey an idea throughout the whole world in less than a second.

So where is society going? What world views dominate thinking in Western society? These are big questions and not ones which I am able to answer satisfactorily. However, my experience of talking to people about the

Christian faith suggests to me that there is a number of cultural presuppositions that impinge on our presentation of the gospel.

One of the most useful ways of grasping these presuppositions is to think in terms of footprints. We have all had the experience of walking along a beach and realising that we are not the only people to have been there. Footprints in the sand reveal other visitors, though they are not all uniform. Some will be very deep while others are shallow, and some will be barely discernible. However, they all make up a tapestry of evidence that humanity has been there.

Much of Western society is like that when it comes to culture. Our society does not just reveal one worldview, one cultural norm, or one way of looking at reality and belief. Rather, history has shaped our society and shaped it again and again. At every point, a cultural footprint has been laid down, and there will be people within our community who bear the hallmark of a variety of cultural signatures. None of these signatures will be universal and there will be a great deal of overlap. Further, some will be more influential than others, particularly in some segments of society. For us as evangelists, however, there needs to be a good understanding of all of them, so that we can effectively reach out to the people that we meet. We should start by looking at the events that shaped Europe as a whole. when the church was first born.

The advent of Popes and prelates

The Christian church was not launched within a vacuum, but rather into a world filled with an enormous variety of religious persuasions, all competing for supremacy. As a consequence of this competition, the early Christians suffered greatly as they shared their faith, giving rise to the expression 'the blood of the martyrs is the seed of the church'[1]. This did not stop them, however, and in time they gained traction, with Christianity becoming the fastest growing religion in the ancient world.

Perhaps the most significant event in the long run was the conversion of the Roman Emperor, Constantine. At the time of the decisive battle of the Milvian Bridge, Constantine had a vision of the Christian God promising

---

1   After Tertullian, who wrote laconically, 'the blood of Christians is seed' ('... semen est sanguinis Christianorum.') (*Apologeticus*, L.13).

victory. He ordered his soldiers to place the Chi-Rho sign (the Greek monogram for Christ) on their shields and they then won a decisive victory, thus securing the empire for Constantine. The following year he imposed an edict of toleration, putting an end to the persecution of Christians and allowing them the same status as adherents of any other faith.

The impact of these moves did more than assist the growth of Christianity; it ultimately made it the official religion of the Roman Empire. Sadly, it became a watered-down Christianity, complete with a great deal of tradition, pomp and ceremony which would not have been recognised by the New Testament writers. The primitive faith of the apostles would morph into the elaborate religion of the medieval Roman Catholic Church and the eastern Orthodox churches. Its impact on Europe, however, would be profound. The Church became so influential that it was almost like a skeletal structure holding the continent of Europe together. When the Roman Empire collapsed, the Church was the most influential power in existence. The Pope could command armies, make kings tremble and form political alliances, such as making Charlemagne the 'Holy Roman Emperor' in AD 800.

By the middle ages the Church dominated all areas of life throughout Europe. It was not just the seat of religious authority; it also had things to say about politics, education, medicine and the arts. Every town had a priest, and his role at the centre of community life was unquestioned. Whatever the Church declared to be true was considered true. People were culturally conditioned not to question the Church's authority. The Bible itself became scarce and virtually disappeared from public life, as the Church took the responsibility to be the repository of truth and to convey what it felt the masses needed to believe. In the darkened gloom of medieval religious life, the truth of the gospel was lost in the fog of tradition.

The footprint of medieval Christianity still exists today, even though it is very much less influential. There are many Roman Catholics and Orthodox Christians whose only real contact with the Bible is through the Church. They put Church traditions on the same level as Scripture and believe whatever their priest says. While the number of communicants drops every year, the attention paid to Popes by the media demonstrates that the Roman Catholic Church still holds sway over the hearts of millions of people all over

Europe and also in the UK, while the Orthodox Churches also command many followers. 1400 years after the coronation of the first Pope (Gregory the Great), a young university student called Gary can stand beside me in Ibrox stadium and tell me that he is not convinced by what I am telling him from the Bible, because his priest thinks differently. This is a footprint that today's evangelist has to reckon with.

The advent of modernity

The dominance of Christendom within western Europe lasted for centuries, but eventually cracks began to appear. The Church continued to be the repository of truth and the revealer of God's will. As hardly anyone doubted the existence of God or the objective truthfulness of the Church's stance on things, intellectually Europe was hermetically sealed. There were, of course, people from other religions living within or near Europe, such as Jews and Muslims. However, given the intellectual and religious stranglehold which the Church had, these belief systems were considered to be false religions and from time to time and place to place their adherents were persecuted. As the 16th century dawned, however, this stable cultural outlook was then shaken by the Renaissance.

At the heart of the Renaissance was Francis Bacon (1561–1626) who is arguably one of the first modern scientists. Bacon emphasized the need for experimentation and believed that the use of the scientific method would lead to new discoveries as well as unify the sciences. He wrote about an ideal world in which science would become the key to a successful and happy society. This idea of the connection between scientific endeavour and a utopian society would be an enduring one.

In the Enlightenment period which followed, theology was superseded by science as the arbiter of truth. Eventually, it was the scientist who was at the cutting edge of cultural thought and not the priest. Whereas in the Middle Ages the Church was the ultimate source of authority, with God at its head, the Enlightenment ensured that human reason was crowned king. The precursor in this revolution of thought was René Descartes (1596–1650). Descartes set out to devise a method of investigation that would discover truths that could be relied upon as certainties. He did this by doubting everything except his own existence. He then affirmed his own existence by the reality of his thought processes. The rationale was that if a person was able to think, then the very fact that he was thinking was proof of his existence. After all, how could thought processes come from nothing? This theory was summed up in his famous expression 'I think therefore I am' (*Cogito ergo sum*). For him it did not matter what kind of thoughts he was having, the very fact that he could think was irrevocable proof that he did exist. This, he claimed, was the starting point in a search for certainty.

Descartes had a huge impact on subsequent thinking. Divine revelation was replaced by human reason as the starting point for knowledge. If someone wished to discover the truth about a particular subject, the surest way of making that discovery was to use rational thought and deductive reasoning. This new way of thinking led to massive changes in all disciplines of knowledge. This could most clearly be seen in the scientific work of Isaac Newton (1642–1727).

Newton regarded the universe as an orderly machine that operates according to observable laws. He was a Christian and hoped that once the universe was understood, those who studied it would be able to wonder at the greatness of God the Creator. Certainly, that was his own experience, but in time the scientific community merely saw their intellectual discoveries as evidence that science and human reason reigned supreme. The modern world, with its irrepressible confidence in science and human reason, had truly begun. Reason would now judge all areas in life from education to morality and theology.

The cultural footprint laid down by modernity has been deep and enduring. The certainty of reason and the monumental development of modern science have not only facilitated enormous human progress throughout the world, but also led to the marginalisation of faith in many parts of culture, not least within the academy. This has become particularly evident in recent years with the rise of what has become known as the New Atheists. This group of intellectuals, which includes luminaries such as Richard Dawkins, Sam Harris, Peter Atkins, Daniel Dennett and the late Christopher Hitchens, are intent on opposing religious belief of all kinds.

The New Atheists are evangelists for atheism. They believe that the case for God is very weak and that science provides sufficient explanation for the origin of life and the universe. Furthermore, they claim that religious belief is actually harmful and that it is to blame for many of the world's ills, including terrorism, the oppression of women and homophobia. Theirs is not the calm voice of the cautious sceptic, but rather the shrill screech of an angry preacher. However, their influence is such that Charles could not listen to a 16-year-old girl preach on Ealing Broadway during the Olympics without rudely interrupting.

From modern to postmodern

Culture never stands still; it is like a pendulum that continues to swing in different directions. In the aftermath of the Enlightenment and the modernist culture that it spawned, another significant cultural change took place, which has become known as postmodernism. Volumes have now been written about postmodernism and many of them overstate the extent to which postmodernism really affects our lives. Some scholars even differentiate between what they call hard and soft postmodernism, in an attempt to explain why some people seem to be postmodern in their thinking and behaviour, yet cling on to some of the assumptions of modernism. Of course, the two are closely related to each other, as a biblical story will illustrate. If modernism with its confidence, its belief in the supremacy of human reason and progress could be compared to the tower of Babel, postmodernism could be compared to the confusion and chaos of the babble that followed God's judgment when there was no common language. But how did postmodernity begin?

It is not easy to state exactly when postmodernism began, but certainly a leading precursor was Friedrich Nietzsche (1844–1900), a brilliant philosopher from a pious Protestant family. It would not be correct to describe Nietzsche merely as a postmodernist, for he really fits into the existentialist camp, but his ideas were remarkably similar to those of contemporary postmodernists.

Nietzsche declared that God is dead, and suggested that once God is removed from the picture, human beings take his place and must recognise that they are responsible for the world. Their role is to do the things that are traditionally expected of God, namely they are to decide for themselves what is true and what is right or wrong. He taught that, without God, there is no basis for any objective values, meaning or significance in life, and this necessitates the abandonment of any concept of objective right or wrong. Morality must be decided by the individual. Nietzsche despised modernists who denied the existence of God, yet retained Judeo-Christian values. It is not that Nietzsche rejected values or morals as such, indeed he realised their importance, but he insisted that we make our own values rather than discover them or receive them from a transcendent Lawgiver.

Nietzsche also abandoned the idea of objective truth, insisting that truth was purely subjective. He stated that it did not matter whether a belief was 'true' as long as it was 'life-affirming', that is, capable of giving those who believe in it feelings of freedom and power. Nietzsche's legacy was to produce a generation of thinkers who thought that human life was of little intrinsic value and that objective truth simply did not exist. This was not the start of postmodernity, but the intellectual conditions which would eventually herald the beginning of postmodernity were now in place.

With an intellectual framework in place, what was now required in order to produce postmodernism was a cataclysmic event that would demonstrate that human progress was a lie and that the elevation of human reason would not bring utopia. In the end, there were two such events: the two world wars which tore Europe apart and heralded a general disillusionment with the modern world. The terrible inhumanity of Hitler and Stalin, and that of later tyrants, put paid to the idea that the modern world was getting better. While science was burgeoning, it was not making the world a perfect place or providing answers to the deepest questions in life. Questions like 'Why do I exist?', and about the injustice of Western economies, and the negative impact that they make on the poorest countries in our world, put further nails into the coffin of modernity. The world was waking up to the fact that science and human reason were failing to deliver clean and uncomplicated progress.

According to most scholars, the cultural shift which took society into the postmodern era took place in the 1960s when many young people began questioning modern civilization, with its social regimentation and technological advances. Gene Veith goes as far as to state that postmodernism began on 15 July 1972 with the demolition of the Pruitt-Igoe housing development in

St. Louis (Guide to Contemporary Culture, p. 39). This trophy of modernist architecture, which was built to be functional, became so impersonal, crime ridden and depressing, that it had to be torn down. The modern world view, with its rational basis and logical regimentation, had become impossible to live with.

A questioning of truth

What then is the net effect of this change in worldview? Perhaps the most obvious contribution that postmodernity has made to contemporary culture is its questioning of absolute truth. In a world dominated by modernism, there was a general consensus that science could provide all the answers and make life better. Our postmodern generation does see the value of science, but recognises that science has also brought industrial pollution, gross inequality and nuclear weaponry. It has benefits, but it also has flaws. The result has been that postmodern man no longer sees science as the thing which will solve all man's problems.

But this questioning has not stopped at the door of the scientific world. There has been a more general questioning of supposed truths, to the point where few are committed to the idea that absolute truths exist. This process has been greatly speeded up by the advent of the global village and mass media. People in the West are now continually bombarded with the cultures and value systems of peoples all over the world. These have inevitably been compared to Western culture and cultural values, and in many cases Western culture has been found wanting. The sheer proximity of other cultures and values has made it socially unacceptable to criticise them, and if anyone dares to, or even to make a robust critique of another culture, they are accused of xenophobia or worse. Increasingly we are developing an eclectic culture where any value or idea can easily be assimilated. What was once considered to be true, correct and normative is now not seen in this way. There are no norms, or to use the language of the French postmodern philosopher, Jean François Lyotard, there are no meta-narratives. It is not so much that truth has been challenged; it is more that there now is no truth in an absolute sense. Truth is merely a matter of opinion.

Downgrading of the Deity

Another result of this cultural change is that God has ceased to be central in people's thinking. In one sense, this is not a new phenomenon. The Enlightenment, and the modernist culture which it spawned, also questioned God. The theory of evolution, developed by Charles Darwin, provided the sceptics with a naturalistic explanation for the life which removed any necessity for God. Science was then free to take the position vacated by God.

The difference in the way God is viewed by the postmodern world is that God is not opposed, he is merely downgraded to a position of anonymity. In today's society, you will find few people who argue aggressively that God does not exist. God has been so devalued in most people's eyes that he is simply not worth arguing over. It matters little, therefore, what view a person has about the existence of God, or what kind of a god he might choose to worship. It will merely be interpreted as his opinion and not some objective reality to which everyone must subscribe.

It is interesting to note that many people in the postmodern world do not reject spirituality. Indeed, many would use tarot cards and crystals, and read their star signs in magazines and daily newspapers. There is also evidence that people are drawn to events to participate in a kind of mass spirituality. According to John Drane, this was exactly what happened at the funeral of Princess Diana. He describes people coming onto the streets and open spaces to mark their grief as a kind of pilgrimage, while others kept vigil by watching the proceedings on television. But these forms of spirituality are not sustained by any concept of objective truth. Rather, they are the kind of subjective, experience-orientated spiritualities that fit neatly into the postmodern holdall.

Relativized morality

The questioning of absolutes has also led to a moral framework that has been relativized to the point where it has become meaningless. No longer can a thing be considered to be right or wrong in a moral sense. Rather, the talk is of lifestyle choices. If someone chooses to engage in a homosexual relationship, or to experiment with recreational drugs, we cannot condemn him as immoral, for there is no moral yardstick by which his actions can be judged.

Any objectors to his lifestyle choice will be dismissed as intolerant bigots. In this way, the postmodern world has essentially abolished sin.

The media propagates this new moral freedom by handing the responsibility for this to the audience, who then decide how morals are constructed. Today's arbiters of morality are the talk-show hosts who canvas public opinion and determine what is right. Oprah Winfrey and others like her will inevitably have much more impact on the nation's morals that any church or institution. In the end, right and wrong will be determined not by any objective moral code, but by the personal taste of the individual. This will mean that morality will be reduced to its lowest common denominator. As long as you don't hurt anyone else, or Mother Nature, then anything goes.

Pluralism

What is true for morals is also true when it comes to religion. If there are no absolutes, then no one faith can claim to be true in an absolute sense. At best, a particular faith can be no more than true for the individual. Though the West is considered to be at least nominally Christian, the reality is that Christianity occupies no more space on the shelves of the spiritual supermarket than any other religion.

In a postmodern world, all religions are equal, and equally true. They must all be taught in school and accepted as valid for those who are practitioners. The only heresy that exists is the suggestion that what someone else believes might actually be wrong. In such a world, evangelism is by its very nature abhorrent, as it presupposes that what another person believes is in some way inadequate. The average man in the street is quite happy for a Christian to have beliefs, provided he doesn't expect others to become believers. Any attempt to convince someone of the rightness of Christianity will be met with questions about why Christianity is any different from any other faith.

In such a world, the Bible carries no authority. Though it is the Word of God, it is not recognised as such. It is no more true than the Koran or Bhagavad Gita. At best, it can only be pious religious opinion, but certainly not the unique revelation of God that Christians understand it to be.

Experience

A further effect of postmodernism is its obsession with experience. Facts have been replaced by feelings and truth by experience. I have already mentioned Nietzsche's belief that an idea did not need to be true as long as it was 'life-affirming'—that is, it gives the person a feeling of strength and freedom. The contemporary maxim, 'If it feels good, do it', says more or less the same thing. Life is not built on objective truths, but on experiences. Our actions should not be judged by any moral yardstick, but by whether we enjoy the experience of living.

It is important to understand that postmodernism is not just a philosophical idea that exists in the minds of an educated elite; rather its footprint in our culture is very deep and its effects can be seen all around us. It can be seen in beautiful shopping centres where the experience of 'retail therapy' is as important as obtaining the goods. Buying things for their usefulness is less important than the image and identity which the commodity can provide. We become worshippers of the iPhone, Bench jeans and Nike blazers. It can also be seen in the music industry, where diversity and self-expression has produced a plethora of styles, from Acid Jazz to Hip Hop and grunge to Ambient Techno. We see the impact of postmodernism in the digital world, where people demand 150 TV channels and watch only 20. It can also be seen in education, where the teaching of historical facts is less important that interpreting the events, and in politics where image and sound bite is a more potent vote winner than substance and policy.

It is the world that Jacob and Hilda inhabit: a world of confusion, devoid of objective values and where the Bible might be respected as a religious text, but carries no weight or authority. As evangelists we need to learn to persevere with people influenced by this footprint, because they may hear our words, but will only be impressed by the integrity of our lives.

The advent of new citizens

One final footprint that makes up our culture is the one made by the many new peoples who have come to settle in the UK and throughout Europe. Immigration is a hot political topic today, and the rise of political parties such as the United Kingdom Independence Party (UKIP) have taken advantage of concerns over the issue. Whatever we think of immigration it is a reality, and will continue to be, because throughout the western world we are not producing enough children, people are living longer, the working-age segment of the population is shrinking. So we need an influx of immigrants to keep the economy functioning. Yet throughout the Western world many are uneasy about it, as the UK referendum, the US presidential election of 2016, and politics in many continental European countries in 2018 show.

Immigration over the past 40 years has resulted in many Christians coming to live in the UK. Some of the largest churches in the country are African or Afro-Caribbean. But it has also resulted in large numbers of Muslims, Hindus, Sikhs and Buddhists coming to live here. The UK is home to almost two million Muslims, and Europe widely defined is home to 44 million. Multiculturalism and religious diversity have placed a large footprint within our culture, and Christianity can no longer claim to be a preferred choice or occupy any more space on the shelves of the spiritual supermarket. Today's evangelists will not only need to know how to communicate the gospel, but also how to nuance their message so as to make it comprehensible to people of other faiths. Like the Turkish diplomat's wife whom I met in Strasbourg, there are many in our culture who respect the Christian faith, but believe it to be fundamentally wrong, for they are devoted to a different world religion. Our presentation of the gospel must be capable of convincing them.

Discussion Questions

1. What examples can you see in your community of pluralism and relativism?
2. How would you convince someone that absolutes in morality really do exist and that we as humans are accountable?
3. What can we do to emphasize the authority of the Bible as God's revelation?
4. How can we witness to atheists, agnostics and sceptics without appearing to have swapped reason for blind faith?
5. How can we proclaim the uniqueness of Christ in a multi-faith society without being offensive?

CHAPTER 3

Coming to Terms with Warp Speed

For those who follow Star Trek, there is a familiar term used in connection with the series' notion of space travel: that term is 'warp speed'. When the Star Ship Enterprise wanted to get somewhere really quickly, or get out of trouble in a hurry, the crew would engage a special propulsion system that would enable them to travel faster than light. As if to emphasize just what this meant, the actors on the set would grab firmly onto a chair or some other fixed object, as they were propelled a great distance in just a few seconds.

This, of course, is science fiction; none of it was real. What is real, however, and also fairly frightening, is the rapid rate of change that has taken place within contemporary society in the West in recent years. Not only have we been shaped by the philosophical changes already summarized, but we have also experienced a dizzying array of other changes, which have come about simply because we live in a world where nothing remains the same. There have been a variety of attempts to warn all of us of this facet of life, one of the most famous of which was the landmark book *Future Shock* by Alvin Toffler[1]. He compared the sense of shock that occurs when things change rapidly to the 'culture shock' people have when they go to live in another country. He notes what a struggle it is when a person finds himself in a place where 'yes' may mean 'no', where a 'fixed price' is negotiable, where to be kept waiting in an outer office is no cause for insult, where laughter may signify

---

1 New York: Random House, 1970.

anger—the result is 'bewilderment, frustration, and disorientation'. Likewise, it is a struggle when you discover that what you thought was contemporary last year is now part of history.

According to Toffler, the main difference with the future shock in the modern world is that, whereas a person experiencing culture shock can return to their native land and be surrounded by familiar things once more, the person suffering from future shock can have no such retreat. It is impossible to turn the clock back and prevent progress or change. It is not even possible to stay the same. While Dr Who has his Tardis and can travel back in time with it; that too is science fiction and not real. In the real world, life hurtles on at a frightening pace and inevitably drags all of us with it.

When my grandmother was alive, I frequently remember her complaining about the way life was constantly changing (to be fair that was not the only thing she complained about!). I must confess that I got fed up with her criticisms of the society in which I was growing up. She seemed to be against everything, from supermarkets to advertising. The way she talked gave the impression that the 'old days' were wonderful. The truth is that in many ways they were not. She grew up in a world where there were few rights protecting workers (especially female ones), where some of her contemporaries had to leave school at the age of twelve and find work, and where many people could afford only one pair of shoes. For her, however, the magic of the old days came not from any belief that life was intrinsically better seventy years ago, but because in those days she was surrounded by things that were familiar to her.

Now that I have more than a few grey hairs on my head, I am beginning to understand a little of the fear that she experienced. As an evangelist, I visit schools where pupils spend much of their time researching by surfing the Net—some are even supplied with their own iPads. I, on the other hand, left school before computer studies became part of the national curriculum, and I find myself constantly trying to keep up with all that is happening in the world of information technology. When I was young, I listened to Elvis, the Rolling Stones, the Specials, KISS, AC/DC and the Undertones. When I mention these names to my children, they do not recognise most of them, and the music they play so loudly in their bedrooms is no more pleasurable to my ears than sticking pins into them. I remember enjoying geography at school, but now find that a modern atlas will not remain modern for long, because of disintegrating empires, young democracies and new sovereign states that want to return to their indigenous roots. Again, my children never use an atlas, at least not if Google Earth is at hand on their laptops; and as for road maps, they are redundant in the world of the sat nav and GPS on the smartphone. Since beginning my working career, I have seen such huge changes in the workplace that I wonder if I will ever keep ahead of the game, despite the benefits of ongoing professional development programmes. The truth is that future shock has begun to set in, and I often struggle not to become as disorientated as my grandmother once was.

The global village

Not only does our world change, but the rate of change seems continually to accelerate. Modern transport has shrunk the world down to a global village. Recently, I flew to Australia to speak at a two-day conference in Sydney. I then had a couple of days off and was back home to Scotland again, all within the same week. Such trips would not have been conceivable just a few years ago. If we were to go back as long ago as 6,000 BC, the fastest way to travel over long distances was by camel caravan, averaging about 8 miles per hour. By 1600 BC, the chariot was invented, taking the speed up to 20 miles per hour, though even then only in short bursts. This continued to be the fastest form of transport for several thousand years. In 1825 the first steam locomotive came into service and it had a top speed of only 13 miles per hour. By the end of the nineteenth century, more advanced engineering had taken the steam locomotive to a speed of 100 miles per hour. These steps had taken thousands of years. In less than sixty years, however, the speed at which man can travel had increased fourfold with aeroplanes in the early 1940's doing 400 miles per hour. By the 1960's rockets could do 4,800 miles per hour and men in space capsules could orbit the earth at 18,000 miles per hour. The far corners of the world are no longer remote. Indeed, they can be accessed in a matter of a few hours and at relatively little cost. Today, there is even talk of bringing samples back from Mars and the possibility of space tourism.

If modern forms of transport have shrunk the world, then television and the Internet have brought the world into our living rooms. We watch films that bring to life cultures from around the globe. As we turn on the news, we are immediately informed about airstrikes in Syria, landslides in Bolivia and the latest sporting events in China. There is even a National Geographic channel that ensures that no part of the world is cut off from the gaze of outsiders. Of course, even *how* we access this information is rapidly changing. The bulky towers of desktop units are becoming a thing of the past, and laptops and tablets fight it out for market supremacy. Even they struggle to keep up, as hand-held or wrist-borne devices become the preferred way of getting information, taking photos and doing banking. Smart phones are increasingly smart, but have a shelf-life of only a few months before the next model is launched. Even a technophobe like me has ceased to buy a traditional newspaper, as I prefer to download it via an app. For me, the most frightening thing about all of this is that by the time this book is printed and in your hands, most teenagers will be smiling smugly about the dated technology that I am now describing!

Linked with these multi-media developments is a huge increase in knowledge. It is estimated that prior to 1500 AD, in the whole of Europe, only about 1,000 book titles were being produced per year. This was due not only to the primitive methods of writing and printing, but also to the knowledge levels of the time. By 1950, Europe was producing 120,000 titles per year. What previously would have taken a century was now being achieved in just a few months. By the mid 1960's, the output rose again to the point where, worldwide, books were being produced at the rate of 1,000 titles per day. Although today more books are being printed faster than ever, the cutting edge of communication and education is no longer the printed page but the Internet. In 2013, a report in *The Guardian* suggested that, in Britain alone, Internet traffic was so huge that it equated to 360,000 e-mails per second, and this rate was growing every month at the rate of 20,000 e-mails per second.

Scientists have also markedly increased in number, in particular over the past one hundred years. In 1910, there were about 8,000 British and German scientists, and these made up a significant proportion of the world's total. By 1980, there were an estimated five million research scientists across the world.

China is now becoming a major force in this field. In 1996, the US published 292,513 science papers, ten times the number of China's 25,474. By 2008, the number in US had increased very slightly to 316,317, whereas in China it had grown sevenfold to 184,080. Chinese spending on science research has reached $100 billion annually, and in 2006 alone China produced 1.5 million graduates in science and engineering. We are now in a situation where China is home to 77 million graduates and India 78 million.

This huge expansion of knowledge has led to increasing specialisation. In my own academic field of religious studies, someone who goes to university will have a huge cross-section of people teaching them, each dedicated to one narrow area of research. I know one professor who only ever researches and lectures on the writings of John, another on 18th century European religious thought, and another on contemporary Islamic theology. My former college principal once joked with me, telling me that the definition of an academic is someone who knows everything about nothing and nothing about everything. It was a joke, but one that does reflect the increased specialisation necessary in a world of rapidly expanding knowledge.

Although technology has undoubtedly made life much easier for many, and lifted the burden of the mundane and routine from many working lives, it has not brought liberation from pressure. Indeed, the modern world economy has increased the pressure that we feel, and has made stress a daily reality for everyone. Terms like 'industrial competitiveness', 'productivity' and 'unit cost' have become part of everyday speech. In every industry, companies are having to work smarter and harder to keep ahead of the game, and this in turn puts pressure on the workers who actually produce the goods. To go into business is to spend many long hours striving to keep up with the competition and fighting for increasingly small profit margins. While it is true that modern industrialised nations are providing their citizens with greater prosperity than ever before, it comes at the price of burnout, stress, broken marriages and neglected children.

In this materialistic rat-race, everyone must deliver productivity and value for money. Professions like nursing and teaching are not immune from this. Go to any high school or hospital, and you will meet dozens of staff members who will tell you that their jobs are much more difficult and less fulfilling than they were twenty years ago. The pressure comes not just from the employer but from the high expectations that we as a society have cultivated over the last few decades. Everyone wants their detached house and expensive furniture. We all want to drive cars with central locking, heated seats, rear-view cameras and ceramic brakes. The luxuries which modern life has provided, like exotic foreign holidays, HD TV, smart phones and designer clothing are now considered to be basic necessities. Without them life is just not worth living. The result is that we work harder and longer to purchase more, even though it does not make us any happier or healthier.

Of course, there is the other side of the coin. While many in our society enjoy a prosperous lifestyle, there are many others who have been left behind. I meet many young people with no qualifications, no job, no prospects and no aspiration. Many of today's young people are destined to spend their entire lives on benefits, and this will in turn create a new 'underclass', where desperation and resignation are the norm.

Human machines

All these changes can make society an extremely dehumanising place. A friend of mine who lives in London describes it as the most lonely place on earth. That hardly seems possible in a city of eleven million people. He works in the 'City', a financial district where some 300,000 business people and office workers ply their trade. Despite being surrounded by so many people, the area where he lives and works is nevertheless full of strangers, who spend very little time talking to each other. Many of his contemporaries are so busy running around hectically being productive that they have little time for one another. What is true of parts of London is true of many big cities through Europe and the West. People do not make friends easily because our society appears not to value interpersonal relationships. We go to the supermarket and take our groceries to the checkout counter and never say hello to the cashier. People like that are human, and individuals in their own right, but society dictates that they are machines, just as the tills are machines. They are there to be productive, not to be befriended. People are no longer people, but voices at the end of the line in a call centre or statistics in the job centre.

What effect do these changes have on the people to whom we are to witness? The answer is that they have a profound effect on how people view life. Our society is full of people whose lives are stressful and preoccupied with many worries and concerns. People also hear all kinds of voices and are subjected to information overload. In such a world, it is difficult to know what is true and what should be believed. This has led many to ask the question, why should we believe anything at all? Our society is also full of people who are so taken up with materialism and the pursuit of happiness that spiritual thoughts barely come into their minds. They are too busy living for the present to prepare for the future. There are also many who cry out for recognition because they feel that they are nobodies.

All these issues need to be taken into consideration, as we go into our communities with the good news of the gospel. We need to be clear in our presentation, so that we do not add to the confusion that people are already feeling. There also needs to be a recognition that people are at breaking point with so many pressures, and that our message must offer them the peace of Christ and a new set of values that will put possessions in their proper perspective. We need to communicate the fact that we are each made in the image of God and are therefore unique and significant individuals, whose every hair in numbered by a loving Father. Our churches need to offer the sense of community which society so lacks. If we recognise these issues, then we have begun in earnest to fulfil the Great Commission.

Discussion Questions

1. What features of modern life make it difficult for people to commit themselves to the Christian faith?
2. What practical steps can a church take to ensure it remains relevant in a fast-changing world?
3. What impact does media saturation have on people's minds and our ability to proclaim the gospel?

CHAPTER 4

Where was the Church when Society crumbled?

Having considered the changes that have shaped our society, we now need to look at the role that the Church has played in all of this. The last one hundred years have been very exciting as far as the worldwide Christian Church is concerned. In some parts of the world the rate of growth of the Church has been staggering. In Latin America, Africa and China in particular, God has been very evident in the lives of millions. The scene in continental Europe, however, has been somewhat different. Statistically, Africa has ten times more evangelical Christians than Europe. Though the Roman Catholic Church is still a respected force across much of Europe, many Roman Catholics are increasingly nominal and apathetic.

If the figures throughout continental Europe give little cause for optimism, those in the United Kingdom are not much better. Statistics show that in the 1930s there were more than ten million churchgoers out of a population of some 45 million, but today the figure has fallen to below six million out of 62 million. The trend is still downward and affects most mainline denominations, with the possible exception of the New and Pentecostal churches. While it is true that many new churches are being formed, particularly because of the Charismatic movement, the mainline denominations, like the Methodist, Anglican and Reformed, are shrinking at a more rapid rate than the new churches are growing, while the Baptist and Independent church groups are more or less static. This can be seen when comparing the demography of churches to that of society at large. In England, there are 25% more pensioners, and 30% fewer people in their twenties in the churches than in society at large.

The influence which churches exert is also declining. One example of this can be seen in the fall of Sunday school attenders. 6,796,000 children attended Sunday school in 1900—about 55% of the child population. By the year 2000, this number had fallen to 530,000, or 4% of the child population. Though Sunday schools are for the most part anachronistic and have been replaced by mid-week children's clubs, this rate of fall is dramatic and revealing, and also shows the dramatic way in which society uses Sunday has changed in the past century.

The reality is that if you put all churchgoers of whatever persuasion together, only 7.7% of the population of the UK attend church on a regular basis and the number is still falling. Even at Christmas time, when church attendance climbs for the festive season, only 32% of the British population can be bothered to drag themselves out to a church. This fall in church attendance has been matched by a growing secularism which should be a concern to every church member. The report on the 2011 census in England and Wales makes sobering reading[1]. The percentage of people who at least nominally call themselves Christian fell from 71.7% in 2001 to 59.3% in 2011. Furthermore, 14.1 million people said they had no religion at all. Norwich was the authority with the highest proportion of people claiming no religion at 42.5%, followed by Brighton and Hove at 42.1%.

These worrying statistics beg the question, why? What has caused practising Christianity in the United Kingdom to perform so badly, particularly over the past century? There was a time when it was the most natural thing for people to be christened, married and buried in church, but now the church has become a minority community in an ocean of ambivalence. Evangelicals in particular are viewed in a negative way. Clive Calver summed it up by observing that evangelicals are perceived to be a right-wing, fundamentalist, sectarian movement which is anti-intellectual, unconcerned about human suffering and imported from the United States[2]. Where did it all go wrong?

---

1 http://www.eauk.org/culture/statistics/whatsyourreligion.cfm
2 Martyn Eden (ed.), *Britain on the Brink: Church and social problems*, Crossway, 1993, p.144.

Slow to wake up

The question is a very difficult one to answer as it is so broad. It is also complicated, because while there has been a general decline, there are still churches that are vibrant and growing, so the decline relates to the other churches that are not doing well. When we look at these other churches, there are certainly some important reasons for their decline and consequently for the overall decline of Christianity in the United Kingdom.

The first thing that needs to be observed is that many churches have generally been slow to respond to the changes that have taken place in society. As we have already noted, culture moves on at an increasingly-fast pace, but churches can often become calcified and tradition-bound, struggling to cope with the new world that confronts them. All too often, Christians have been answering yesterday's questions rather than tackling today's. Churches have been guilty of holding onto structures that are well past their shelf-life. In short, many churches have struggled to wake up to the 21st century.

The symptoms of this sleepiness are easy to spot. First, there can be an obsessive loyalty to old hymns and traditional forms of worship. Of course, many old hymns are wonderful and timeless, and are used well in churches today. Others, however, do not relate to our generation and neither do the tunes which they are sung to. In one sense, the songs we sing in church are a small part of the overall package, but in another sense, when churches doggedly refuse to make use of the many contemporary worship songs that today's writers are penning, and when they ignore the flourishing creativity in worship that has been a blessing to many Christians, it shows that their whole attitude is one of unwillingness to relate to contemporary society.

Then there is the type of services we hold. The Bible grants a great deal of freedom to churches as far as their structures are concerned. There is no one biblical way of doing church. However, some churches use the same structures and methods that they did fifty years ago, even though people's lifestyles and attitudes have changed markedly over that time span. The structure of a church should be adapted to suit the needs of the people, rather than expecting everyone to fit into the programmes.

There is also the way in which we do our evangelism. Sleepy churches do not ask whether or not their evangelistic strategy is effective, often because they do not actually have an evangelistic strategy. Evangelism is just done the way it has always been done. The only rationale behind this approach is that it worked in the past, though increasingly it is the very distant past. The point is that it was in the past that it worked, not now.

In all these areas many churches have struggled to relate to a changing world and have suffered in the process.

Struggling with liberalism

A second major reason for the overall decline of practising Christianity in recent decades has been the struggle with liberalism. The rise of biblical criticism within the theological faculties of our universities has made its impact on the church. Many of the assumptions that had long been accepted by the Church were beginning to be questioned.

Among the issues that began to divide churches was that of the doctrine of Scripture. Evangelicals have long held to a belief in the inspiration and inerrancy of scripture. In academic circles, however, the Bible was being cross-examined, both in relation to its textual basis and the extent to which it included mistakes. Methods of higher and lower criticism were being imported from Germany and causing many scholars to doubt, among other things, whether Moses wrote the Pentateuch. Philosophers and theologians such as Immanuel Kant, Frederick Schleiermacher and Adolf von Harnack, reduced the Bible to a human book, corrupted and in need of re-drafting and reinterpreting.

It was inevitable that such issues would percolate down to grass-roots level. Though many evangelical scholars began to engage with critical scholarship, it was too little too late. A popular perception arose within society in general that the Bible was unreliable and could not be trusted to communicate God's truth without error. Many people who had never read the Bible for themselves would nevertheless have argued that the copying of texts from generation to generation meant that inconsistencies were common. The Bible was no longer held in reverential awe. To many it was a flawed book, and the debates on inerrancy that went on in the universities and between church leaders only fostered this view. With confidence in the Bible eroding, the

Church found it increasingly difficult to tell people that there was a message from God that they had to listen to.

Denominationalism

Yet another reason for the decline in the Church has been the problem of denominational division. We now live in a world where different denominations appear to be sprouting up everywhere. Recent statistics suggest a total of over 34,000 Protestant denominations worldwide, and in Britain alone the number is nearly 300. This has done little to promote the idea of a united body of Christ and many unchurched people have become confused with the vast array of different churches which apparently offer a slightly different slant on the same thing.

In a very real sense, in this respect, evangelicalism has been its own worst enemy. Jesus prayed in John 17: 20–23 that all believers might be one. The model that he used for unity between Christians was his own relationship with the Father. He commented that the world would be able to know that he had come from the Father because of the unity of believers. Not only have Christians been divided, but their differences have all too often been broadcast to anyone willing to listen. This denominationalism has caused a great deal of damage and driven many away from churches.

Holy island

Local churches have also become isolated from the community. There was a time when everyone got married in church and wished to be buried from there. The Church was the guardian of the nation's morality, and when church leaders spoke they were listened to by the community at large. Even at grass roots level, the local vicar was one of the most respected members of the village. Not so now! The Church, more often than not, is seen as an out-of-touch and out-of-date institution that commands little respect. This has been exacerbated by the sex-abuse allegations that have been levelled at many Roman Catholic and Anglican priests in recent years, and are not unknown in other Christian groups. Church leaders no longer hold sway in the community, as they once did, and the Church as a whole makes little impact on the moral conscience of the nation. In short, the Church has slowly lost its grip on society.

Confusion about the gospel

A more recent challenge relates to how we understand the gospel and how it is lived out. Over the past couple of decades, a movement grew up within evangelicalism that became popularly known as the Emergent Church. Like any movement, there was a broad spectrum represented. Some Emergents were hugely creative, and even experimental, in the way they did church, but they were theologically orthodox. I would celebrate their efforts and would see it as a very positive contribution to the evangelical world. Some Emergent leaders, however, made and continue to make significant efforts to distance themselves from a conventional evangelical stance and this has led to concerns as to their view of the gospel. The doctrine of the atonement has been questioned, as has the doctrine of hell. Some have suggested that other religions might have value and might be valid pathways to God. In terms of lifestyle, some Emergents have suggested that being a practising homosexual is not incompatible with being a committed Christian. While the Emergent Church is now past its peak it still continues, along with other expressions of Christianity that it birthed. All of this has caused a significant amount of confusion and has been a distraction for many churches, and as a consequence they have not been able to communicate the gospel with any clarity.

Defined by culture, not counter-cultural

Another problem which many churches have faced is that they have tended to reflect the values of their culture rather than living radical counter-cultural lives. Often when this has happened, they have justified their position by claiming to be relevant to their communities. However, there is a big difference between being relevant within a cultural context and imbibing that culture. We show true relevance by preaching a clear gospel, but in a way that is comprehensible, engaging and attractive to people in that culture.

This imbibing of cultural values can be seen in many ways. One of the most obvious is the way in which many churches today interact with and imbibe aspects of postmodern culture. Postmodern culture abandons any concept of objective truth. As we have already noted, for many people it does not matter whether or not an idea or belief is true, as long as it is enjoyed by the person who believes it. In that sense, everyone can hold onto their own truth and not feel threatened by others, because all ideas or beliefs are considered equally true.

Within some churches, there has been the tendency to downgrade truth in deference to the views and opinions of others. As a theology lecturer, I have sometimes been accused of fostering division, because of my insistence that the Bible is true and its truths are non-negotiable. Some Christians have even suggested to me that the study of theology actually dampens spiritual ardour and prevents Christians from simply enjoying their relationship with God. When I hear these views espoused, it becomes clear to me that some Christians have indeed imbibed postmodernity into their Christian experience. Whether or not our culture denies the existence of absolutes, the fact is that they do exist. God, who is the ultimate reality, has revealed himself in Scripture, and every word is inspired, true and to be believed.

If the Church refuses to build its life and existence on the sure foundation of Scripture, if we do not insist that truth exists and must be lived out, then the consequences will be dire indeed. We will end up with a Church that believes nothing and is willing to compromise on anything for the sake of harmony. Such a Church will not be in a position to call people out from the crowd to follow Jesus, because it will have blended in with the crowd and will have become indistinguishable from it. Christian doctrine is essential, because it is the truth that separates us from those who do not follow Jesus Christ or live a God-honouring lifestyle, and this, by definition, is what it means to be holy. To water down our doctrines, to treat them as though they are negotiable, is to state that we no longer want to be a holy people, acting as salt and light in this dark world.

Furthermore, in a postmodern society where everybody's opinion is valid, society is fragmented and divided into a series of 'taste communities', each with its own beliefs and ways of doing things. There is no sense of continuity or overarching ethos that binds us together. Again, some churches are falling for this idea that everyone within the church should be allowed to express their own spiritual life in their particular way. Such churches create different types of church services for the different taste groups within their congregation.

In practice, this means that those who enjoy lively worship will go to the lively services, while those who are naturally more sombre will go to the more sedate services. While there is need for variety within the life of the church and it is valid for the differing needs of people to be met at an appropriate level (for example teaching done in an all-age Sunday school), there must nevertheless be a tangible expression of the body of Christ within the local congregation. God did not just call lively people to repentance, or people who enjoy a particular type of music. God called young, old, sedate, energetic, doleful and expressive people to repentance. It is not God's intention to divide us into different 'taste groups', but to unite us by his Spirit into a community where love, tolerance and mutual respect reign. It is precisely when I worship with other Christians who have different personalities and outlook from myself that Christ is glorified by our oneness in his name.

Postmodernity is also based on feelings and not facts. It is the experience and not the reality that counts. Something is said to be good if it feels good. Logic, rationality and objective right and wrongs are ditched in favour of what can be enjoyed. Once again, some churches are in danger of swallowing the dangerous drug of postmodernity. When worship is judged by how it makes the worshipper feel, as opposed to the extent of consecration in the life of the worshipper, then worship has sold out to postmodernity. When biblical exposition and deep theological thinking are replaced by interesting stories and entertaining presentations, then postmodernity has entered the pulpit.

I am not suggesting that our worship should be devoid of emotion and our preaching dull. Quite the reverse! I am just as concerned when worship is no more than a cerebral exercise, for that is modernity, not Christianity, and just as much a danger in church life. I am also very much in favour of creativity when preaching. But there must be substance as well as well as sound-bite; otherwise superficiality will rule.

This having been said, it will also be important that we engage in meaningful dialogue with people. The environment that people are increasingly coming from is one in which questioning rather than certainty is common. The rejection of absolutes has led to the need for dialogue and working things through. This often results in questions being left unanswered and loose ends left untied. For Christians who like being dogmatic about their beliefs, and who like to have their theology highly systematised and neatly packaged, this is a difficult thing to handle. They associate questions with unbelief, and therefore take a dim view of the questioner.

Stuart Murray suggests that today's churches need to be 'communities where doubts can be expressed without fear or censure, where people can explore their uncertainties, rather than toeing the party line'[3]. He notes that Thomas was not rejected when he doubted the resurrection of Christ, but was nurtured back into a position of faith. This policy may have its dangers and may be an uncomfortable thing to live with, but given the uncertainty and doubting that so pervades our society, there seems little alternative. We need to be able to embrace people as they make their first tentative steps towards faith, and be willing through nurturing to build up their faith, while allowing them a sense of belonging in the church community. Young Christians, and even those who have yet to commit themselves to Christ, need to feel that they can raise issues and express doubts without feeling alienated or rejected. My own experience of Christianity is that I have been able to grow and develop as a Christian, despite at times having major questions that I struggled to find answers to.

Discussion Questions

1. Why do you think Christianity grows so rapidly in the developing world and less so in Europe?
2. Describe what church decline (if any) has taken place in your area?
3. How can we counter liberalism and denominationalism in the life of the church?
4. To what extent should we gear our church services to peoples personal tastes and what parameters should govern our decisions?

---

3 Stuart Murray, *Church Planting*, Carlisle: Paternoster 1998, p. 185.

CHAPTER 5

Witnessing from the Margins

I often feel that I have missed my vocation and that I should have been a statistician. I love numbers and data and trying to extract meaning from statistics. They help to build a picture of the way life really is, which is often very different to the way we would want life to be. When it comes to statistics about church life in the UK, or anywhere in Europe for that matter, the numbers do not lie and frankly they make worrying reading. This is because the statistics clearly demonstrate a decline in Christianity and an increase in both scepticism on the one hand and other world faiths on the other. One of the dangers of reading statistics on the state of the Church in the UK is that they not only inform, they also demotivate. When we observe the decline, it is easy to feel that all is lost and that reaching out to such a fallen society is just impossible. Thinking this way, however, would be a mistake. This is because our perspective should be tempered by a number of important factors.

First, as we look at the statistics, we need to bear in mind that much of the decline that we see in the Church has been because people who were nominal in the first place have now lost all interest in Church. In many ways, this is not actually a bad thing, because it means that those who are still at church are committed, and churches are actually healthier as a result. This sifting process can be a benefit, because a small church full of committed and motivated Christians is in a much better position to grow than a church full of people who don't care very much. If some of the decline is because people who never had a committed belief have now left church, then this is not a stark and absolute decline. Rather it is a refining of the church that will make the situation less complicated in the long run.

Secondly, while some Christians may look wistfully back at the halcyon days when the medieval Church dominated life in Europe, and wish that we could return to that period once more, it is actually important that we view the Church at that time for what it really was. Certainly it is true that centuries ago most people went to church and the Church exerted a significant influence on all of society. However, the Church in the medieval period and beyond was actually riddled with corruption, greed, errant theology and a lack of vibrant spiritual life. The Church was bigger, but not purer. Often people went to church not because they had a living relationship with Jesus or because they wanted to experience God's power and presence in their lives, but simply because it was the culturally acceptable and required to do so. The rise of Christendom, for all its apparent outward success, was actually something very shallow. There were of course many true believers who loved God and demonstrated that love by the way they lived their lives. But there were many more whose spiritual lives were mere ritual, and who did not experience a true transformation brought about by the power of the Holy Spirit. Indeed, even the medieval clergy were often devoid of any real spirituality. We should not wish to go back to those days, but rather we should wish for a genuine faith that makes a difference to the whole of a person's life.

Thirdly, we would do well to look at the early Church and their context. This is important because the early Church seemed to have much to contend with. Christians were a despised and marginalised community. They were a people without influence and without public recognition. Persecuted by the Jewish religious authorities and Romans alike, the early Church found itself under great pressure from the outset. The first generation of Christians were Jews who rapidly found themselves unwelcomed by the Jewish community. After the martyrdom of Stephen, when persecution became systematic and organised under the direction of Saul of Tarsus, these Christians found themselves fleeing to strange places, hoping for some sort of sanctuary. Despite the danger they were in, however, they did not shirk away from their responsibility to share their faith. On the contrary we read that they 'preached the word wherever they went' (Acts 8: 4). Through their witness, and latterly the witness of Paul the apostle, the gospel was embraced by gentiles. These gentile Christians also found themselves under pressure from persecution and had to live out their Christian lives under the suspicious gaze of their own hostile gentile communities.

When Peter wrote to a disparate group of Christian churches in his first epistle, he described them as exiles (1 Pet.1: 1). He also described them as strangers, foreigners and aliens (1 Pet. 1: 17; 2: 11). It is clear that Peter assumed that they would be outcasts in a world that did not acknowledge Christ. He goes on to recognise that they have had to suffer all kinds of trials (v. 6), but interestingly he tells them that these trials would prove the genuineness of their faith and bring glory to Christ (v. 7). Peter's words hint at the real hardship that early Christians had to suffer and their continuing marginalisation within the Roman world. Their troubles were not going to go away, indeed the hostility towards the Church would eventually lead to the horrors of the Coliseum in Rome and the other arenas of the Empire, where hundreds and possibly thousands of Christians would die cruel deaths to entertain the crowd and their callous rulers.

With such opposition and marginalisation, it would seem unlikely that the Church could grow and make a significant impact within society, but that is exactly what did happened. Even in the face of persecution, these early Christians boldly proclaimed their faith and eventually won huge numbers of converts. The Church was to become the fastest growing faith in the Empire. The clear lesson for the Church today is that we should not give up, even if all the odds seemed stacked against us, for it was from a position of real weakness that the early Church grew. Life in the margins is not the end. The Church can not only survive, it can also thrive from the margins. As Tim Chester and Steve Timmis state, 'From the margins we point to God's coming world and offer an alternative lifestyle, alternative values and relationships—a community which proves incredibly attractive'[1].

Of course, in order for us to have this perspective and also to take advantage of the situation that we find ourselves in, we need to think differently.

---

1 Tim Chester and Steve Timmis, *Everyday Church: Gospel Communities on Mission*, Wheaton IL: Crossway 2012, p. 40.

Many Christians still think they are in a Christendom era. They expect people to come to church if invited, and they assume that if the gospel is presented to people, they will both understand and want to become Christians. They work on the basis that a Judeo-Christian worldview is self-evidently true and valuable, and are not sure what to say or do when they come across people whose worldview is vastly different. What is more, they assume that biblical ethics should be the norm for society as a whole, and so will campaign for these values to be universally applied. Indeed they get so caught up in campaigning that they sometimes forget to evangelise. The problem with all of this is, of course, that we live in a post-Christendom era where the rules are very different.

This difference is shown in the fact that we as Christians are a minority. We do not have the right to demand privileges that are not available to any other minority group, and we should not expect to be treated differently. What is more we are, as already stated, aliens and strangers (1 Pet. 2: 11). We live in a culture that is not Christian; indeed it is hostile to Christianity. It is not surprising, therefore, that there are many aspects of our culture that we find uncomfortable and challenging. We will not feel at home in this world, because we are not at home. We have no power to control our society, or to compel it to be the kind of society we would like it to be. We are only able to change it by proclaiming the gospel and seeing individuals transformed by its life changing power. Our message is only one among many on offer within our society, and we must demonstrate its veracity by our lives and the credibility and coherence of our presentation.

None of this should discourage us. Like the early Church, if we have a conviction that God is with us and that faithfulness and courage will be rewarded, then there is reason for optimism. In the case of the early Church, their success came out of a position of weakness, and therefore weakness need not necessarily be a negative. Indeed, it is the teaching of the New Testament that God's strength is brought to bear in the context of our weakness (2 Cor. 12: 9). Weakness is our secret weapon, because it is when we are weak that we throw ourselves on the mercy of God and rely utterly on him.

It is possible that the Church will always be in the margins, certainly here in the UK. However, if that ensures its purity and utter dependence on

God, then the margins is a good place to be. What we need to ensure is that the margins do not become a ghetto. While we are a despised minority, we should not shrink back into ourselves for the sake of preservation. Our role as Christians is to go out into the world and proclaim Christ. We go out as sheep among wolves (Matt. 10: 16), but we go out in the power of the Holy Spirit.

Discussion Questions

1. Are there any benefits in the church being at the margins? If so what are they?
2. What do we need to do if we are to thrive in the margins?
3. How do we instil a sense of confidence in Christians who feel marginalised and are afraid of being witnesses?

CHAPTER 6

Talking Softly, Speaking Clearly

I have a friend who is a back-slidden Christian. In truth I cannot be sure that he ever genuinely committed his life to Christ, but certainly at the moment he is not following Christ, and there is little evidence that the Christian faith has ever impacted him. By nature he is a cynic, so whenever we meet up the conversation is interesting, to say the least. He once asked me what I was going to do over the summer, and I told him that I would be leading a team of young people on an outreach in France. He was not particularly surprised by this, because he knew that I work for GLO and that as an organisation we are involved in short-term mission. Nevertheless, his cynicism got the better of him, and he just felt the need to say something negative. He began by saying in a rather arrogant tone, "Now, let's get this straight". I knew right away what he was about to say. He continued, "You, as a Christian evangelist, are going to go to a place where you have not been invited, to preach a message that no one wants to hear, about a faith no one is interested in, and you are going to demand a change that no one actually wants to make; but you will do it all because you think you are right—even though everyone else thinks you are wrong".

Had he not been a friend, I might have got upset and felt hurt by his comments. After all, my reason for going to France was because I love the people there and wanted them to know the love of God in their lives. Having said that, I also knew he was right. People generally don't want to hear the gospel and neither do they want their lives to be changed, at least not the kind of change the Bible talks about. What is more, when we do evangelism, it is not usually because people have asked us to evangelise them, rather we take the initiative; and often when we talk to people about our faith, they would rather we didn't.

This context must surely temper how we present the message to people. We need to remind ourselves that many people in our society consider Christianity to be irrelevant; some even find it objectionable. They see no reason why the Christian faith should be considered any more true than any other religion, and consider that morality is an arbitrary thing and a personal choice for the individual, not a universal guideline for all. Whether we like it or not, Christianity is a minority interest, and as we try to communicate it we will encounter a range of obstacles. They must not prevent us from evangelising, but, in doing so, we need to take them into account.

Convicting without criticising

The first obstacle that we face is the sheer ambivalence towards, and even incomprehension of, sin that many people have. For many people in our culture, morality has been relativised, and consequently the idea of sin is hard to get across. Most people will have some sort of moral code, but unless they have some religious or philosophical commitment to ethics (which some do of course) this moral code will be reduced to the lowest common denominator. In effect, the only sins that exist are those of hurting other people, hurting nature, or being judgmental, which of course is a charge often levelled at Christians. In a world like this, it is important that we demonstrate that sin really does exist and that some things really are bad. We also need to point out that sin is not just terrible crimes such as murder and child abuse, but also includes such things as impure thought, improper speech and false motives. The only way to do this is to demonstrate that God is creator, and therefore we as his creatures are morally accountable to him. God has objective standards which are culture-transcending and apply to every human being. We may not like God's standards, but it is he who sets them, not us. Our job is to obey, something that the human race has singularly failed to do.

Communicating this difficult point presupposes that we have had the opportunity to talk to our non-Christian friends at some length. The problem is that, as the previous chapter has indicated, most non-Christians never go to church or engage in meaningful spiritual dialogue with Christians. Later on, I will deal with how we get alongside non-Christians to share this message, but for now it is important that we take on board this important point. We need to learn how to convince people of the seriousness of their sin without appearing to be self-righteous, judgmental or arrogant.

Hurdling pluralism

Another obstacle to communicating the gospel centres around Christian belief in the uniqueness of Christianity, or more specifically the uniqueness of Christ. Jesus was unambiguous when he said, 'I am the way, the truth and the life, no one comes to the Father but by me' (John 14: 6). The problem is that in a multi-faith, pluralist culture, such claims of uniqueness are perceived as arrogant and extremely offensive. Often when I have been speaking to non-Christians about the Christian message they have replied, "Well what about Muslims and Hindus? Are they not going to heaven?" The difficulty is that if I were to say, "No", I would be branded an offensive bigot, but if I say, "Possibly", I cease to be true to what the Bible teaches.

This is a difficult question, but it will frequently confront us if we are serious about evangelism. We need to learn how to communicate the truth of the gospel without demeaning other faiths or the sincerity of those who hold them. I am not suggesting that we capitulate to pluralism, for that would be entirely wrong. There is only one way to God and no true Christian can deny that. Our presentation of the gospel must leave people in no doubt that Jesus is the only way of salvation and the only way to access God. But we must bear in mind the cultural sensitivities of those to whom we witness, tread with caution, and express ourselves carefully and sensitively on this topic.

Cerebral Christianity

A third obstacle can be that Christianity is rooted in history. The Christian faith is based on certain historic facts, and it is true because these facts are true. However, many in our society are so experience-orientatcd that they will be turned off by a gospel presentation that relies solely on fact. People are not looking just for something to believe in, but also something that they can experience. They don't want just to know things about faith; they want to feel them as well. Christianity will appeal to many in our society only if it is seen to work in everyday life.

I am conscious that so often my evangelistic preaching depends on a dry presentation of information that feeds the mind but does little else. Sometimes I have been asked if I enjoy being a Christian, or if I think that my faith helps me to live my life in a better or more fulfilling way. Those who ask these questions are not disputing the essential historicity of what I have told them, but they are interested in the difference that Christianity makes to me experientially.

Again, I am not suggesting that the facts of the Christian faith are irrelevant. Indeed, I find Christianity satisfying because, among other things, I know it to be true. But Christianity needs to be felt and make a practical difference! For all the dangers in an experience-based faith, it is important for me, and I suspect every Christian, that my faith makes a difference to my home life, my work life and my social life. It greatly influences and shapes the roles I play in life, such as husband, father, work colleague and friend. Psalm 34: 8 says, 'Taste and see that the Lord is good'. The psalmist, having personally experienced God's power in his life, invites others to do so too. As we communicate the gospel to our experience-orientated generation, we need to demonstrate that Christianity is not only objectively true, but that it also makes life qualitatively better. Jesus can help a person's marriage, bring greater meaning and purpose to their life and bring them into the remarkable experience of knowing and loving God.

Biblical illiteracy

A fourth obstacle that we face is biblical illiteracy. Because Christianity has been so marginalised in western society, and because the Bible is not treated with any sense of reverence, for most people the Bible is a book to which they have never turned. If the average person in the street owns a Bible, it will probably be gathering dust in some remote cupboard. More likely, they will never have owned a Bible and will rarely have heard it quoted.

I find it intriguing, when I watch TV quiz shows, to see how badly even well-educated people handle biblical questions. On one recent TV quiz show, a man was asked which Bible book comes after Genesis. Clearly he had no idea and so mentioned the only other Bible book he knew, which was Revelation. I smiled smugly, because having come from a Christian family, I could have correctly answered that question at the age of five. But that lack of knowledge of the Bible is not uncommon. Indeed, I suspect that most people in the United Kingdom would not have been able to name another Bible book.

When it comes to evangelism in this culture, lack of biblical knowledge is a big barrier. We will need to find a way of communicating meaningfully to people who know virtually nothing about God, the origin of sin, or the person of Jesus Christ. We will need to assume nothing, and get into the habit of starting any conversation at the basics.

A model for evangelism

How do we begin to communicate the gospel in such an environment? What should be our starting point? Perhaps the most helpful lessons I have learned have been derived from the techniques of some of the biblical evangelists. The foremost of them was Paul, and the book of Acts reveals a great deal about his evangelistic strategy. One of the most helpful passages for me has been Acts 17: 26–38, which records Paul's experience in Athens. I will mention it briefly now and then develop it further later on.

We need to remember, of course, that the culture that Paul was dealing with in Athens was a very different from today's in the United Kingdom; but, as Don Carson points out, there are also some striking parallels[1] To begin with, the Athenian culture was pluralistic and a far cry from a Judeo-Christian world view. What is more, in Athens, Paul was addressing a group of people who were utterly biblically illiterate and therefore knew absolutely nothing about the God of the Bible.

The first thing to note is Paul's assessment of the culture. Luke tells us that Paul perceived the city was 'full of idols' (v. 16). Considering the kind of city that Athens was, this was a remarkable observation indeed. Athens reached its

---

1 D.A. Carson, *The Gagging of God: Christianity confronts pluralism*, Grand Rapids, MI: Zondervan, 1996, p. 496.

heyday under Pericles (495–429 BC) and then declined as a military power, finally being conquered by the Romans in 146 BC. Nevertheless, it was a world-famous city, renowned for the splendour of its buildings, statues and monuments, and as a place of learning. Athens had been no less than the intellectual capital of the world. In the ancient world, there were three great university cities, Athens, Tarsus and Alexandria. Of these, Athens was the most prestigious. It was the home of the great dramatists and philosophers, the cutting edge of culture and education. Into this great city came Paul. He was not overawed by the grandeur of the architecture, nor was he taken in by the highly-developed cultural life or the sophisticated philosophy, though all of these were impressive. Rather, he became deeply distressed by the fact that these people were fallen and idolatrous.

We also need to learn to critique the culture in which we live and view it through Christian eyes. It is easy for people living in the West to associate the mission field with parts of the world like Africa, Latin America or the Far East. However, the world has changed greatly from a spiritual point of view over the past couple of centuries. Africa, which was described as the 'Dark Continent' by early missionary pioneers, now has ten times more evangelical Christians than Europe. Ethiopia, where I grew up, was once a missionary-receiving nation, now it has as many Christians as, put together, France, Germany, the United Kingdom, Italy, Spain, Poland, Portugal, Switzerland, Ukraine, Russia, Hungary, Austria, Belgium, Bulgaria, Serbia, Moldova, Greece, Turkey, Denmark, the Czech Republic, Slovenia, Slovakia, Belarus, and the Netherlands. Sometimes we can become so absorbed with the technology, education and the cultural sophistication of the West, that we forget that in reality people in the West are permissive, idolatrous and morally decadent. The impetus for evangelism comes as we critique our own culture through Christian eyes and see how spiritually desperate it really is.

Notice also that Paul begins to witness in the synagogue, as was his custom, but then goes out into the 'market place day by day' (v. 17) to witness to those who were there. The reason for this is obvious. Only a few Athenians were likely to enter the synagogue, so if Paul confined his evangelism to the synagogue he would only reach the few. To reach the many, he had to get out to the market place. The market place was the centre of public and business life; therefore, it was the most likely place to meet people. Of course, it would have been much more comfortable for Paul to do his evangelism in the synagogue, surrounded by things that were familiar and by people who shared his basic worldview. However, Paul knew that evangelism is not about what makes us comfortable, but rather what will reach others. He therefore went beyond his comfort zone to bring people the gospel.

In much the same way, we need to think about our market place and how we can begin to rub shoulders with people in natural situations. Bearing in mind that only 7% of people in the United Kingdom attend church regularly, the 93% who remain will need to be reached in some way other than through a church service. This situation is unlikely to change; as Tim Chester points out 96% of children in the UK are growing up without any exposure to church or its message[2]. If the majority of people are to be reached, we need to stop thinking of evangelism as being something that is done only in a church service, and begin to think of it as something that is done 'outside' of the church building.

Paul's message

Once Paul aroused some interest, he was invited to present his case at the Areopagus, which was the chief court and main administrative body in Athens. His address shows how he communicated the gospel message. Paul begins by noting that the Athenians are 'very religious'. He was not complimenting them for their religious beliefs; indeed, patronising comments used to win an audience were not tolerated in the Areopagus. Rather, he was beginning to build a thought-bridge between the biblical position and theirs, by establishing some common ground. In short, he was being sensitive and courteous, so that he would be in a position to bring the gospel to them.

The same kind of presentation is required today. With all the confusion and doubt which our culture is causing, it is simply not tenable to proclaim the gospel from a distance. Preaching at people will not communicate the gospel: it will simply alienate them and heighten the sense that we are different

---

2 Tim Chester and Steve Timmis, *Everyday Church: Gospel Communities on Mission*, Wheaton IL: Crossway 2012, p. 29.

from them. Rather, we need to establish some common ground which will then lead to the presentation of the gospel.

Several years ago, I was talking to a young man on the streets of Copenhagen, where I was preaching in the open air. From the outset of the conversation, it was clear to me that he was full of doubts about God and struggled to believe in any absolutes. Rather than condemn his sceptical world view, I built a bridge to his position. I made the comment that he seemed to be struggling with the Christian message and its intellectual credibility. Then I told him that I had experienced many doubts about Christianity before becoming a Christian and that, even as a Christian, I went through times of doubting the accuracy of the Bible and biblical history. This surprised him, but increased his interest. We then talked about some of the areas where we were most liable to be sceptical: for example, the historicity of the resurrection. The bridge between us was beginning to be constructed. I then told him that I was now completely satisfied with my Christian faith, because many of my most troubling doubts had been answered. This simple technique not only enabled me to go on to explain what I believed, but why I believed it. In short, I was able to share the gospel with him and explain why the gospel is intellectually credible and defensible.

Having established a bridge, Paul then mentions the altar to 'an unknown god' (v. 23). This kind of altar was common in Athens, so Paul's audience would easily have identified with what he was saying. He uses this inscription as a means of introducing to them the true God, who is unknown to them. This was a powerful object lesson and demonstrates one of the reasons why Paul was so successful as an evangelist. It was because he spoke their language. He ensured that he presented God to them in a way that they could understand.

This is something else that today's Christians need to learn. It does not take long for someone who goes to church to pick up a great deal of jargon. So much of the vocabulary and so many of the expressions that Christians use are incomprehensible to people who are unchurched. We get so used to using this religious jargon that we do not even realise we are doing it. It is vital, therefore, that we find object lessons and modes of expression that will enable us to communicate the gospel to our peers, so that they fully understand what we are saying to them.

One of the exercises which I set my students is to write out their testimony and a short gospel presentation without using a list of the words that I write up on the board. Included in this list of 'banned' words are 'sin', 'saved', 'born-again', 'personal faith' and 'cleansed'. These words are perfectly good and convey a great deal of theology to someone who is a Christian and knows Scripture, but to someone who is unchurched they can simply be confusing. Even Jesus had to define what he meant when his use of the expression 'born again' confused Nicodemus, a leading theologian. To someone who no longer believes in absolutes or has a vastly different worldview, the whole concept of sin will require explanation.

Next Paul goes on to explain who the true unknown God is. He deals with the question of creation (v. 24), establishes the fact that we as human beings are accountable to God, and asserts that God wishes to have a relationship with us (v. 27). But then the crunch comes in verse 30! Having built bridges and ensured that he is speaking in their language, Paul ultimately had to challenge the false notions held by the Athenians. They were idolaters, and this needed to be dealt with. Though Paul was preaching in a culture that was highly pluralistic, he did not succumb to it.

I believe that Christians need a great deal of courage today, if they are to truly communicate the gospel in our multicultural, pluralist and relativistic society. Though we need to demonstrate love, understanding and grace as we interact with our non-Christian friends, this should never be at the expense of presenting the uniqueness of Christ as the only saviour of the world. The only way of getting to heaven is through the person of Jesus Christ, and those to whom we witness need to know this. We need to hold our nerve and insist, gently but unwaveringly, that salvation comes only as a result of Christ's work on the cross. Paul knew when to play the diplomatic card and when to dig his heels in and contend for the truth, and this is a skill that we need to develop in our witnessing.

It is also significant to note at what point Paul brings Jesus into his message. What Luke records for us is obviously an abbreviated version of Paul's sermon. Paul talks about God as creator and builds an entire biblical worldview before he mentions the person of Jesus Christ. This might seem strange, as the gospel is about Jesus and his death on the cross. But there are reasons for Paul speaking in this way. Suppose he had begun his sermon with the statement, 'Jesus Christ is the Son of God'. This is a perfectly good theological statement, that we as Christians know to be true. The trouble is that his audience would not have had the capacity to understand what this meant. Someone in the crowd may well have shouted back, "OK, but of which god is he the son?" Coming from their perspective, these people had no idea of who God was. Therefore, anything which Paul might have said about Jesus would have made very little sense. Jesus and his death on the cross are meaningless without a knowledge of God, humanity and their relationship to God, the fall, and the incarnation. The Athenians knew nothing of this, and so Paul had to do some preparatory work before coming to the climax of his message, which was obviously God's answer in Christ.

In much the same way, we need to be careful about our assumptions. When we are witnessing to people who do not go to church or have no consciousness of personal sin, even sound theological statements will not register, because the foundation is not in place. When we talk to people who claim to be atheists, or perhaps agnostic, it makes no sense to talk about the uniqueness of Christ, because they neither appreciate the significance of the incarnation nor are they able to accept that anything exists outside of the natural world. When we talk to people from other religions such as Islam or Hinduism, the work of the cross is incomprehensible and they do not grasp how this event could be the response to God's wrath. Many of the evangelistic Bible study booklets that I have used over the years are based on the assumption that the users will have a Judeo-Christian worldview, will know who Jesus is and will understand that we need to deal with the problem of our sin. This is increasingly unlikely to be the case. Many unchurched people do not have the faintest idea what the Bible teaches about God and his world. That being the case, John 3:16 and other verses that we use in evangelism may not be enough. A better method of communicating the gospel might be to start by using the book of Genesis to build up a foundation upon which verses like John 3: 16 can then make sense.

Don Carson tells the story of a missionary friend who went to India[3]. After his language study, he spent a decade travelling around numerous villages preaching the gospel. Many people made professions, but they were only adding Jesus to the long list of deities that they were already worshipping. No churches were planted and few made any real commitment to God, as he was unable to break through the deep-rooted pluralism of Indian culture. Following a furlough in which he did a lot of soul-searching, he returned to India to concentrate on just two villages. This time, he began with the doctrines of God, humanity and the fall. The result was quite different. There were fewer professions, but two churches were planted. The difference was that on his second time round he made no assumptions and built a foundation for belief. This, it seems to me, is exactly what we need to do in our pluralistic society in Britain.

Discussion Questions

1. How do we achieve the balance between speaking relevantly into our culture and yet at the same time being faithful to Scripture?

2. Christianity should appeal to people's hearts as well as their minds. What can we do in our gospel proclamation to ensure that both these aspects come through?

3. How can we convince people of the seriousness of their sin and the reality of God's judgment without alienating and offending them?

4. Paul went to the marketplace to share the gospel. What is your marketplace and how can you begin to share the good news there?

---

3   D.A. Carson, *The Gagging of God: Christianity confronts pluralism*, Grand Rapids, MI: Zondervan, 1996, p. 502.

CHAPTER 7

Filling the Credibility Chasm

I spoke to Ryan on the streets of Motherwell, Scotland, some time ago. I was with a group of students from Tilsley College who were attending my lectures on evangelism, and as part of the course we decided to hold an open air meeting in the local shopping precinct. It was a good conversation, and Ryan was very happy to talk about his own belief system, as well as listen to what I had to say. He lived locally, and when he told me where he worked I was delighted, because I knew a Christian who worked in the same place. I mentioned this person to Ryan, hoping that it would further build a bridge with him, but sadly this was not to be. Ryan knew that the man whom I referred to was a Christian, and indeed the man had on more than one occasion told Ryan that he needed God in his life. Unfortunately, I discovered from Ryan that the man was unkind, selfish and bad tempered in the workplace and that no one respected him for his faith.

Having thought about some of the issues involved in evangelism, we now need to think about the kind of people we need to be if we are to be effective evangelists. The story of my conversation with Ryan illustrates this point well. If evangelism is based on relationships and getting alongside people to share the good news, then our lives will be in full view of those to whom we are witnessing. People will not be impressed merely by the message being given to them, but will need to see the message being lived out in the lives of Christians. It is not sufficient in this experience-orientated culture to communicate the facts of the gospel: Christianity must be seen to work and make a difference. This can be done only if we, as Christians, are living holy lives with real integrity in front of our unchurched friends.

Absence of hypocrisy

The first thing that we need to ensure is that the life we lead is consistent with the faith we claim to hold. People are not stupid. To coin an expression, if we don't walk the walk, we can't talk the talk! Talk that is not backed up with a genuinely Christian lifestyle will be unconvincing, shallow and unappealing. My experience of 'friendship evangelism' is that the people to whom I am witnessing get to know me very well, and therefore putting on a mask of Christianity will not work. My life must be consistent, through and through. As someone wisely commented to me, 'A man's pious words carry no weight if his behaviour is inconsistent with them.'

I have been to South Korea several times and have visited the border with the North. On each side of that border there is a military barracks to keep out unwelcome visitors. On the south side, this barracks consists of a few humble buildings. On the communist north side is a glorious and very large building that can be seen for many miles. The reality, however, is that the building is no more than a facade. Viewed from the side, it goes back no more than a couple of metres. Christians can live such a sham. Their Christianity is only skin deep. This kind of lifestyle impresses no one and will do irreparable damage to the cause of Christ. In Romans 2: 21–24 Paul criticised the Jews for their hypocrisy, stating that the gentiles were blaspheming God as a result. It was ironic that it was people who claimed to follow God who were the ones who dishonoured God's name, rather than those who did not believe in God. If Christians are inconsistent, they can cause their non-Christian friends to become cynical about the Christian faith.. On the other hand, a life that displays Christ-likeness (Gal. 5: 22, 23) will earn respect.

A living relationship with Christ

The second thing that we need to ensure is that we have a living and active relationship with Jesus Christ. It is said that you become like the company you keep. This is certainly the case with me. I come from Belfast, but have been living near Glasgow for the past twenty-three years. Over that time, my accent has slightly moderated, without my even realising it. I have begun to use expressions that are thoroughly Glaswegian and sometimes even say them with a slight Scottish lilt. When I take a short trip back to Ireland, my Belfast accent returns with full force. Again, it is because of the company I keep.

The same thing applies to the spiritual life, which is why Christian fellowship is so important. In our relationship with Christ, if we spend quality time with him, it shows in our life. People can see a perceptible change in our attitudes and conversation. This demonstration of Christ-likeness will be an invaluable asset in evangelism, because it shows those whom we are trying to reach what a change Christ can make in a person's life. I know one couple who have become Christians in the past few years. He became a Christian first, which was a shock to his wife, as neither of them had ever had any interest in faith, indeed they both had an instinctively negative view of Christians. Not only was she taken by surprise by his conversion, but she became angry and resentful towards him because she felt his new-found faith was a betrayal of her. Despite this problem, he lived out his faith within the home and, as time went on, she began to notice that he became a more caring husband, a more attentive father and a more gracious friend. She concluded that his faith was not a mere fad or religious commitment, but it was something that transformed him and made him a better person. In time, she became so impressed with his Christ-likeness that she also became a Christian.

There are other reasons why this living relationship with Christ is so important. For a start, you cannot encourage others to commit themselves to a relationship with Jesus Christ if that is not your own day-to-day experience. To do so would be hypocrisy. It is the reality of our relationship with God that is so convincing. During times when we can't answer all the questions that are put to us, it is our living testimony that adds weight to our claims. Though we should not run away from the intellectual challenges brought against Christianity, the reality of what Christ has done in our lives this week is just as convincing any argument.

What is more, a life that is transformed by God is a very attractive one. I well remember the reason why I became a Christian. Although I knew I was a sinner and had heard many convincing presentations of the Christian message, this knowledge formed only a small part of the reason why I made my commitment. The main reason was the lovely Christ-likeness I saw in the lives of other Christians. I had the great privilege of coming into contact with a group of young Christians who were deeply spiritual and fun to be with. The reality of their faith could be seen in everything they did, and I found myself wanting what they had. It was from this point that I made a commitment to Christ that enabled me to experience all the joy which these role models had. Their Christ-likeness proved to be like a magnet drawing me to Christ himself.

The fact is that, in much the same way as a bad Christian can turn people off Christianity, a good one can make people want to become Christians. This can only happen when we really are walking closely to Christ and allowing his qualities to rub off on us.

Integrity

Part of Christ-likeness is having personal integrity. This is such an important point that it merits a category of its own. I have a friend who is a pastor. When I first met Bob and saw him in action, it made me wonder what qualified him to have such a high profile and responsible position within the church. He is not the best preacher I have ever heard—indeed on the rare occasions that I have heard him, I found his style to be a little boring. What is more, he displays very few overt leadership qualities. Certainly, he is a caring man and that is a great quality to have in the Christian ministry, but he simply does not have the charisma or strength of character to make his ministry dynamic.

Then one day, while having a conversation with one of Bob's friends, I discovered the reason for his esteemed position within the church. His friend told me that Bob was someone who was utterly trustworthy. He was a man of such integrity that Christians and non-Christians alike would trust him with their lives. Whenever Bob spoke people listened, not because he was a great orator or persuasive debater, but because whatever he said was the truth, the whole truth, and nothing but the truth.

When our non-Christian friends see how we live and hear what we say, they will form opinions of us. If we have given the impression that what we say needs to be questioned, or if our actions don't match what we profess to believe, then they will find it more difficult to accept the gospel. If, on the other hand, they find that we are utterly trustworthy, then when we begin to share our faith with them, they will be compelled by their own estimation of us to listen carefully to everything we say.

Peace in crisis

A final quality we will need, if we are to be effective witnesses, is the ability to be at peace, even in a time of crisis. We live in a world of change and uncertainty. Many people struggle to cope with all the implications of change. For many people, life is about frayed nerves and troubled minds. On top of the struggles of modern existence are the personal crises that many people have to face. Someone loses their job, a teenager goes off the rails and gives his parents sleepless nights. A sudden death brings devastation to a family, illness brings almost unbearable stress. These crises are commonplace and affect nearly everyone at some point or other.

For Christians, too, life can have its painful moments. But the difference for us is that we have a relationship with the God who controls, not only our lives, but the universe as well—a God who is loving, merciful and wants to help us through all the difficulties that life forces us to confront. David wrote Psalm 3 when he was facing overwhelming odds, as his son Absalom rebelled against him. Even though there seemed no way out of the situation, David was still able to sleep calmly through the night, without being afraid of the terrors that would confront him when he woke up the next morning. This was because his faith was real and alive. It sustained him during his moments of crisis.

This kind of reliance on God demonstrates the reality of the Christian faith. As friends observe us, not only in the good times, but the bad times as well, they can see the hidden strength that a relationship with God can bring. When Christians who are suffering or going through some kind of trauma are able to rejoice and remain positive, it makes an indelible impression on those who see what is going on. This sense of calm begs the question, why? Why are Christians so positive, when their lives are sometimes so awful and full of suffering? One friend of mine who exemplified this recently was a young married man and father of a lovely baby girl, who discovered that he had a malignant growth in his brain. Everyone who knew him was shocked and saddened. However in the face of such bad news he told all his friends, many of whom were non-Christians, that he believed God was completely sovereign in the situation and that he would be content about whatever God's will was. The peace he felt and communicated to others was a great witness to God's sustaining power, and gave him real credibility as he shared the reality of his faith with others.

Discussion Questions

1. What qualities do you expect to see in the life of a committed Christian and which of these do you find most difficult to live out?

2. Which of the above challenges do you find most difficult to deal with in your own life and why?

3. What practical steps can you take to become the kind of person who can witness with credibility?

CHAPTER 8

Beginning at Base

As we reflect on our communities today, the most basic question we need to ask ourselves is: how can we reach people with the gospel? Having an enthusiasm and commitment to the gospel is not enough: we need to think about how that can be communicated to people who do not yet know Christ. The answer to this question is not a simple one, and the decline of many churches is testimony to the challenge of doing evangelism today.

However, once we begin to look for an answer to this question, we will end up with two basic methods of evangelism. The first of these is church-based evangelism. This could be defined as a method of reaching people using church facilities and an organised group of church members. Simply stated, church-based evangelism seeks to reach people with events that centre on a corporate presentation of the gospel, with the church taking a high profile. It has already been stated that many people, even if invited, will never darken the doors of a church, so our evangelism strategy can never be confined to church-based activities. Nevertheless, they do have a place and it should be our natural starting point. We need to be serious about church-based evangelism and make sure that when we do it, we do it well, so that it can be an effective component in our witness.

There are many church activities that fit into this category. These include all-age services, youth and children's clubs, junior church, discovery courses, one-off evangelistic events and friendship outings. Each of these church-based evangelism methods can be very useful, but only when they are carefully thought out. There would be value in writing a whole chapter on each of these methods, but space does not permit. Instead, I shall just list them, adding brief comments on the questions and issues that we will encounter, and tentatively suggesting ways in which we can make the most of them. I do not claim to be an expert in any of these areas; but my comments stem from observations I have made as I have seen others successfully utilising these methods in evangelism.

All-age service

The most basic example of a church-based activity is an all-age service (sometimes also called a family service). Most churches use all-age services as a major part of their evangelistic strategy. While they have much to commend them, they have the obvious limitation of requiring church attendance, and therefore they will not work unless there is a proactive approach to inviting people to come. On the other hand, if someone was to become a Christian, they would need to become part of the church community, which involves attending church, so an all age-service can be an important entry point to church life (though some who have become Christians from the cultural background which I have described in the earlier chapters may well need earlier stepping stones, like an informal, home-based nurture group, before they can cope with a larger church event).

At their best, all-age services provide a welcoming atmosphere which enables visitors to feel relaxed and at ease. We need to bear in mind that no matter how friendly a church might be, or how persistent its members are in inviting their friends, only a small proportion of people will ever come to a service like this. The all-age service should therefore be used in conjunction with other events, and there should be a range of methods used to invite visitors to attend.

In planning all-age services, there are a number of very basic questions that need to be asked. First, how often should a church hold a family service? This question is actually quite important, and the answer is less obvious than one might think. As most churches are accustomed to thinking about church services on a weekly basis, they automatically assume that their all-age service must be a weekly event. There is nothing wrong with this, and if a church finds that a significant number of non-Christians come on a weekly basis, then there may well be good reason for holding it weekly. However, there are other considerations that might need to be brought into the equation. For example, if a church struggles to get people in the community to attend weekly family services, it may be wiser to have them less frequently and put more effort into both inviting people to attend and putting together a service structure that will be absorbing and will communicate effectively.

I know one church that holds an all-age service on the first Sunday of every month, and this pattern suits them. They have a fresh format each time and often link the theme with big events that are happening on the national or world stage. I know another church that also does a monthly all-age service, but they find that a Saturday night is a better time to invite people than a Sunday morning. In my own church, Liberty Community Church, we have a Bible teaching service every Sunday morning, and we hold what we call 'guest services' only a few times per year. We choose special occasions such as Christmas, Easter and Remembrance Sunday to have these services because visitors are more likely to come on those occasions. It is also possible for a church to put a special effort into inviting people if all-age services are not held weekly. Often it is possible to link the all-age service with other things that a church is doing. In one church that I visit, they have a football team which operates as an outreach to men. Twice a year, they invite the football team, along with their wives and girlfriends, to their all-age service and have a spot in the programme to talk about how the team is doing. This idea could apply to many church activities. In the same church, they have a successful children's ministry, and they also link this with their all-age service twice a year, making the children the focus of the service.

Another question that needs to be asked is how an all-age service should be structured. Discussions might need to take place as to whether or not communal singing should be part of the programme and whether there should be any preaching. Again, these issues are important and there needs to be a rationale behind everything that is done during the service. It is the shop window of the church and will leave all visitors with an impression of what the church is like.

My personal preference is for both congregational singing and preaching. I like communal singing because, although it will be alien to unchurched people, it is nevertheless an important part of the lives of Christians, and if it is included, potential converts are introduced to an aspect of Christian living. Music also touches us emotionally, and powerful music accompanied by theologically profound lyrics provides an excellent learning environment that many non-Christians find meaningful. I have heard testimonies where people have referred to songs that helped them grasp spiritual realities and led them to Christ. Clearly, worship in the form of singing can have an important role to play. An alternative could also be to have songs being sung by a band, choir or individual musician. Again if done well, this can be impacting.

My commitment to preaching within an all-age service stems from my conviction that it is still a method of communication, which if well done, is very effective. There are few things more motivational or absorbing than a good preacher passionately and urging his audience to respond to God. Preaching has often got a bad press, but if it is good preaching, it should not be shunned. A good preacher can not only unpack Scripture well, he can also bring emphasis through emotion, timing, expressions and a sense of urgency. I recently preached at an outreach service in a church near my home. In the audience was a man who was completely unchurched. My passage was Romans 1, a powerful chapter in Paul's great epistle which deals with the issue of the fallen-ness of our society. I preached with all the directness and passion that I could muster and wondered what he would make of it all. Afterwards he came up to me, gave me a thumbs-up and said, "Great speech mate, that really touched me". I don't know how much of the message he really understood, but he certainly knew that we were dealing with weighty issues and the impact on him was obvious.

Yet another question is what kind of communication methods should be used. This is down to personal choice and resources, but I have found that using video, PowerPoint presentations, drama, corporate readings, and physical symbols and actions can be very effective in communicating different aspects of the Christian faith. The preaching can then draw everything together and focus the hearers' minds on the challenge of the Christian faith. In my own church one Easter, we built a large wooden cross and placed it at the front of the church. I preached a short message on the cross, and the forgiveness and healing which it offers. We then passed out envelopes, pieces of paper and pens' and invited members of the audience to write down sins or problems which drag them down and then seal them in the envelopes. Next, they were encouraged to get out of their seats and nail their envelope to the cross as a symbolic gesture of finding help and release in Christ. I was glad to see not only church members but also visitors, some of whom were not Christians, come to the front and nail their envelopes to the cross. Such actions are not gimmicks, but powerful challenges to which people can respond and, in responding, draw near to Christ.

Sometimes it can be useful not just to reshape an all-age service, so that you can add value to what is being done, but to have a completely different kind of all-age service. One recent innovation in this regard is 'messy church'. One way of defining 'messy church' is to say that it is a way of doing church for families (and others) using crafts and art, celebration and eating together, all in a relaxed 'family-type' atmosphere. Another definition would be to say that it is church with the emphasis on fun and creativity. The timing of a messy church event will be based on what best suits the whole family. Certainly, it is designed to appeal to the needs of people on the very fringes of church, so that they can get involved in an accessible and non-threatening way.

Messy church has several advantages. First, it targets the whole family. Many churches have the problem of Sunday school children whose parents never attend church. Messy church aims to bring parents and children together. Second, it is flexible, often happening during the week or on a Saturday. Third, the programme is based around discovering spiritual truths as a family rather than as individuals.

There are, of course, drawbacks. Messy church will appeal to families with young children; but single people and couples whose children are young adults may well be less interested. The very nature of messy church means that, while the Bible is taught, it happens at a particular level, so messy church is best used as an added activity, rather than a replacement for core church services. Because of this, while messy church is useful, it is a bridge—a means of evangelism, rather than church in the full biblical sense of the word. And people who become Christians as a result still need more feeding, which will involve taking part in more conventional church services. In practice, churches that use messy church often do it monthly or periodically rather than weekly, and this often fits in well with a church's overall outreach programme.

Of course, all of this presupposes that there will be people willing to attend an all-age service of some sort. As I have travelled around churches in the UK, I have often been struck both by the creativity with which many churches present the Christian faith, and by the lack of hearers. There is little point in putting together an imaginative programme if there is no one to listen for whom the programme has been devised. For many churches, therefore, the main task is to ensure that people actually come to these services.

There is no simple way of getting unchurched people to come to church. Personally, I think that newspaper ads and mass leaflet drops are of some, but only limited, value. I suspect that only one person in a thousand will respond to a leaflet and one in ten thousand to a newspaper ad. Certainly that would be average for the area where I live. How then do we get people to attend? One word sums it up: relationships. The kind of people who might come to an all-age service are those who have some kind of contact with the church. That being the case, if every member of the church would invite colleagues, neighbours and friends to a service, the actual numbers of unchurched people coming to such services would certainly increase.

The problem is getting Christians to invite their non-Christian friends. In practice, this does not often happen. First, because many Christians have few close non-Christian friends, and second, because Christians often make a strong demarcation between their 'secular life' and their 'church life'. Many Christians are vibrant in church, but when they get back to the factory floor or their social circle, they say very little about their faith or church life. This mind-set needs to be changed and church members need to make friends with non-Christians. If they were to be more open about their faith and bring it into conversation naturally, they would have a much greater opportunity of bringing others to church. However, this whole process will not happen until churches begin to teach their members to be salt and light in their community and to see their non-Christian friends as lost people who desperately need to hear the gospel.

In addition to these relationship contacts, it is possible for churches to develop further contacts with people in the community. In my church we have had several youth and children's clubs. Most of the young people who attended them came from unchurched families, but as they came along to our clubs a contact with their families already existed. A few people in our church sat down and thought about how we should develop these contacts. The first thing we did was to visit these homes, 150 in all, and offer them a copy of the Jesus film. Because they knew about the church through the clubs, a high percentage of these families took the film and many said that they enjoyed it. We then began to produce a monthly church bulletin that contained details of all the church activities, as well as a thought for the month. Each month a group of people from our church visited each of these homes with the bulletin. We employed a friendly, non-threatening approach. The purpose of these visits was not to preach the gospel to the people, though if conversations arose naturally we made the most of them, but rather to develop the contact and show a friendly face. These visits enabled us to get to know some of the families well and this has resulted in many of them coming to our guest services. This was just one way of developing contacts; lots more could be thought about.

A church could have a Facebook site and encourage people in the community to become 'friends'. Church members can get involved in local community activities. In our area there is an annual street fair, and we have sometimes had a church stall where we do free crafts with the children, give out church balloons, and sell Bibles and relevant Christian books. Another church I know constructs a float each year for the parade that takes place as part of their town's annual gala day. The point is not how a church builds relationships, but that it does build such relationships, and as a result is able to bring non-Christians to an all-age service.

Age-centred clubs

Another form of church-based evangelism that is widely used is what could be described as age-centred clubs. The most common forms of these are children's and youth clubs, though senior citizens' clubs are also fairly common. Obviously, the different age groups represented will determine the kind of club that is formed, but the basic ingredients tend to be the same. They consist of a mix of social activity and spiritual input.

Generally speaking, most churches do very well when it comes to children's clubs. Even small churches with little gift and few resources can run them successfully. It is more common for churches to struggle with clubs for teenagers, young adults and for people in their thirties and forties. Each of these is quite specialised and needs to be thought through carefully, but I will make a few general remarks about them all.

One of the problems of conducting a youth club is that there is a high casualty rate of young people, even before they get to their teenage years. They may have attended a children's club, but because they do not have a relationship with the leaders of the youth club, they simply do not go to it. This gap has to be bridged. It can be done either by leaders being involved in both clubs or by a half-term feed in between the two clubs. Perhaps both need to be considered. Certainly, there needs to be a strategy that links all the clubs being run, so that no one falls between them. Youth leaders need to be continually reminded that it is all about relationship. Young people these days have constant access to computers, smart phones, video games, contemporary music and any range of sporting activities they desire. No church will have the finance to be able to 'entertain' a group of teenagers. What will keep young people coming to a club is if they have a genuine relationship with the leaders. This relationship is also tapered. Younger teens are happy to develop a relationship with leaders in the context of a larger group. As they get older, however, the need for intimacy, confidentiality and depth of relationship increases. The youth leader will need to make the time to meet with them individually or in small intimate groups.

Youth clubs can be difficult to run because teenagers like to express themselves, thus often creating discipline problems. It may well be that accountability and discipline need to be thought through. If not, the club will involve a great deal of policing and not much communicating the gospel. Incentives are also useful. In one of the clubs that I have worked with, we take the young people on outings: for example, going to a football match or even doing a weekend together. These outings both build relationships and provide a motive for good behaviour.

When all is said and done, the most important thing that we can give to young people is Scripture. This must be done, and creativity is the key. We have found that if the Bible is presented in an imaginative way, using video, drama, discussion and object lessons, it is not difficult to get a group of unchurched teenagers to sit and listen for half an hour. We should not forget the use of technology here either. Young people are constantly in touch with each other, sending texts and Facebook messages, tweeting and sharing blogs or using instagram. My 22 year old daughter can receive up to 100 texts in a day, and while the messages are short and often apparently trivial, she nevertheless communicates with her friends in this way as an expression of their relationship, and she is able to process all of this information. Youth leaders need to realise the potential for using electronic media. I have found it is possible to teach theology, give good counsel and establish a rapport with a young person, using only my smart phone as the means of communication.

Camps and weekends away are also very useful, as they take young people out of their context and into one that is conducive to hearing the gospel and bringing them to the point of commitment. Again, relationships are of the utmost importance, as the leaders role-model the Christian life for the young people. Positive role models can be hugely effective in winning young people for Christ.

When it comes to running clubs for people in their twenties and thirties, a number of major obstacles need to be overcome. First, life is very busy and pressurised, so time is a valuable commodity. If you are a family man with a busy job, there is little time for anything else. Many professional people come home exhausted at 7:00 pm and then need to spend some time with their families. Going to some church activity is the last thing on their mind, especially if they have no spiritual interest in the first place. That being the case, it may well be unrealistic to think of having a weekly activity. It is also increasingly difficult to reach people the older they get. Life's responsibilities, personal hurts, the general scepticism that pervades our society, and the tendency to settle into a personal way of life and thinking, mean that many people will be dubious and, perhaps, even antagonistic towards Christianity by the time they reach their mid-twenties.

On the other hand, there are two factors in contemporary society that will enable churches to get alongside people in this age group. First, our society puts great importance on recreation. The huge proliferation of sports clubs and hobbies is evidence of that. What is more, in this age of depersonalising technology people need to interact and socialise. Both of these factors can be utilised by the church.

One thing that often brings people together, especially men, is sport. Many churches have got involved in football, and even in a church league, as a way of relaxing and enjoying time with non-Christian friends. I play football every week with a group of about 20 men from my town, most of whom are unchurched. It would be wrong to say that this gives us regular opportunities to share the gospel. However, it does bring us into genuine contact with these men, and in the context of our relationship to share something of faith. My prayer is that the relationships that we build will one day enable us to effectively communicate the gospel to these men in a way that we have never had the opportunity to do before. Likewise, a group of men from my church arrange trips to the cinema to watch the latest blockbuster, and the idea is that we invite some non-Christian men to join us also. Often we go out for a meal afterwards and faith can be discussed as part of the general conversation. The key thing here is also to have good role models. A Christian man who is open about his faith, unintimidated by criticism and also able to relate well to other men, can be a very powerful evangelistic tool. The same applies to women. If we can relate naturally to non-Christians and build their trust and friendship we can, in time, win many for Christ.

Creativity is important here. Think of ways that connections can be made. Sport is good, but so too are other hobbies. In many churches, craft groups, and mother-and-toddler groups, have done much the same thing. Some churches have also successfully organised father-and-son clubs or mother-and-daughter clubs. The idea is to develop an activity or hobby that the parents can do with their children. One church that I have worked with had a swimming pool not far from the church building. They began a father-and-son swimming club that proved to be very popular in the local community, not least because it provided an opportunity for fathers to spend quality time with their sons as well as make new friends.

Again, the gospel will not always be presented in a very upfront way, but the friendships that are developed in these activities will enable the Christians to share the gospel informally with their non-Christian friends. The secret to success in such ventures is developing the knack of gossiping the gospel. When persecution hit the early Church, as recorded in Acts 8, the Christians literally had to scatter in all directions. They did not have the time to organise evangelistic events, but what they did do was to 'spread the good news' wherever they went (Acts 8: 4). It was this spontaneous evangelism, to which the Church as a whole committed themselves, that contributed to the great success of this evangelistic endeavour. Today, as individual Christians use the opportunities presented to them within any club that the church forms, the gospel is shared without any 'formal' presentation of the truths of Christianity.

Event evangelism

As well as these regular activities, there is a whole range of one-off events that churches can organise in order to make contacts and deepen friendship. In some cases, there may not be a specific evangelistic thrust in these events, but they provide a setting in which Christians rub shoulders with unchurched people and witness naturally. As a church, we organised a 'paint-ball' outing to reach and make contact with unchurched men. It may seem to be an unlikely evangelism event, but it proved very successful. It was the kind of activity that attracts men of all ages and promotes group bonding. We went through a succession of five battle zones, with a coffee break in-between. By the end of the evening, we had made friends with several unchurched men, some of whom came a few nights later to an outreach meal. During the mock battles, we were aiming our paint guns at each other, but the real aim, which was to get to know each other in an informal setting, was constantly at the back of our minds. The evening was a big success, and made contacts which we are still following up.

There are many less boisterous events that can have the same impact. Some churches organise craft fairs or car-boot sales, in order to befriend people. Others organise activities in their local school and hold a prize-giving in their church during a family service. We have held community talent nights in our church, and these have also worked very well. On a number of occasions, I have also been involved in organising an interactive Passover celebration, complete with Israeli wine, unleavened bread and roast lamb. I have also organised a book club, and have mixed relevant Christian books in with secular ones. These events go down well with unchurched people and provide a natural access point to the Christian faith. Sometimes these events can be structured and have a specific aim in mind. Our church has organised parenting classes and also a 'drug proofing your kids' class. Like many parts of the UK, our area has its fair share of one-parent families, and parents who are struggling to bring up their children. Parenting classes helped both to reach people and also to offer a service to the community. If done well, classes like this can become an important building block in an evangelism strategy.

Another type of event which I have seen used well is a music café. Like some of the things mentioned above, music is something that many people enjoy and is therefore a natural draw which can be used in evangelism. One of the great benefits here is that this medium can be very flexible. Not only can lots of different kinds of music be used, but also for different purposes. Some Christian bands and musicians are overtly evangelistic, both in their songs and their overall presentation. There is a real place for this and it can be used to great effect. However, others have a different kind of impact. The performers write songs about life in general, embracing politics, economics, popular culture, human relationships and meaning in life. The importance of this is that they provide Christian comment on life, and this is a subtle but powerful way of opening up people's minds to spiritual realities. One church that I go to organises regular music cafés on a Sunday night. There is no preaching, and the musicians who come along vary between those who do not openly say they are Christians and those who share their testimonies and their faith overtly. It has proved a great way of enabling Christians to mix in a relaxed way with non-Christians. The church building is set out like a café and food is served. The ambience is excellent for the development of friendships which are being built up and lead to real conversations about faith.

Whatever the event, if it brings Christians into contact with non-Christians in such a way as to develop friendship, and if the Christians are prepared to take every opportunity to gently share their faith, then it will be a success.

Discovery courses

Another form of church-based outreach that has proved to be successful is the discovery course. Some of these courses, like the Alpha Course and Christianity Explored, are ready-made and can easily be utilised by churches. In some cases, it may be more appropriate for a church to develop its own course. For example, at one point we were in contact with a number of people who appreciated our friendship but were very sceptical about the Christian faith. I, therefore, wrote a course that focused exclusively on apologetics, so that the major objections to the Christian faith could be dealt with in detail.

There may also be times when a course like Christianity Explored might be too overtly evangelistic, so a more pre-evangelistic course is needed, one which just raises general issues of lifestyle and spirituality. These courses can then lead to a more conventional discovery course. However a church may wish to proceed with this type of outreach, it has a proven track record.

This type of event has a number of benefits. First, it brings non-Christians into a Christian atmosphere on a regular basis over a period of time. Second, the time given enables the Christian message to be explained systematically and with clarity. Third, it provides the opportunity for feedback and for any questions and doubts to be dealt with. Fourth, it takes attenders from the stage where they are vaguely interested in Christianity to the point where they are being challenged to make some kind of commitment. Fifth, courses of this kind can evolve naturally into discipleship classes, once someone has made a commitment to Christ.

There are a number of key elements in this type of course. Those who attend need to feel at home, otherwise they will not keep going until the end of the course. Alpha courses are centred around a meal, and this is one reason why they work so well. Eating out is a social activity that enables people easily to form friendships and build the relationships spoken of earlier. A meal, as part of a church-organised course, has the same effect. If there are not the facilities to put on a full meal, finger buffets work equally well. Using a hotel or restaurant may also be an option, albeit the cost would be much higher. Having said that, there is no reason why you cannot charge people for coming. Often people feel better about paying for their meal, rather than being given one for free. It is also possible to have a dual purpose, and use the meal as a fundraiser for some good cause which in itself will be an attraction.

There are several important rules to observe when laying on a discovery course. It is important, first, to have people who can competently lead it. These events are informal, but informality can descend into chaos if not well regulated. The leader needs to be able to command an audience, and humour can also be an advantage. Friendliness and warmth are also a must. Second, it is important to ensure that Christians are mingling with non-Christians, so that as much can be communicated outside of the 'main talk' as is done during it. All too often I have attended events in which all the Christians sit at one table and the non-Christians sit at another. This will never lead to good interaction, so always choose people from your church who mix well when you run a course. Third, deal with any questions and issues that emerge honestly and frankly. This is not easy, because the same difficult questions seem to recur. People will ask about the authority of the Bible compared to other religious texts, why God allows suffering, why God's doesn't allow homosexuality and why God would send people to hell. Ducking these questions will not help, so it is important to be prepared to deal with them. Finally, engender the kind of atmosphere that will make visitors want to come back again and again.

Halfway events

In addition to these activities that generally happen in a church building or in the homes of Christians, there can be other events and initiatives that are clearly linked with the life of the church, but which are very non-threatening and often focus on the felt needs of the community. For example, there are different exhibitions that churches can utilise as a form of outreach. Christian organisations, such as Counties, have useful exhibitions for this purpose.

One example is *The Life Exhibition* (lifeexpo.co.uk). This is a multi-media experience using interactive tablets, graphic panels, films and songs to teach primary school children about the story of Jesus. Since its launch, thousands of primary school children, as well as significant numbers of adults, have visited the exhibition. They are guided through the story of Jesus—his birth, teachings, miracles, death and resurrection. The exhibition is split into four zones, each taking a different theme and finishing up in the Life Café, where they relax with a drink and a snack and take part in an interactive quiz, which helps them reflect on their experience of visiting the Life Exhibition. The Life Exhibition can be used in a church building, but groups of churches can also work together, using a central building in their town or city, which could easily be a civic building. The fact that it also covers a part of the RE syllabus makes it a popular choice for teachers, and therefore schools can get involved.

A second exhibition run by Counties is *GSUS Live* (gsuslive.co.uk), which is a mobile classroom which visits secondary schools across the UK, providing lessons on important issues, such as fear, forgiveness and rejection, and helps pupils to discover how Jesus is relevant to their lives. The GSUS Live classroom is kitted out with a multi-media computer suite, complete with motorized touch-screen computers which rise out of tables. Just like the Life Exhibition, the GSUS Live exhibition is run by church volunteers. Churches that use GSUS Live have found that it develops links with the local schools.

Another resource which has proved very helpful to churches is Christians Against Poverty (CAP). This is a debt-help service, aimed at supporting those in most need. It runs money management courses in partnership with local churches, which help people to budget, save and prevent themselves falling into debt. Many churches have found that working with CAP enables them to express the love of God to needy people, and the evangelistic spin-offs have been very significant.

It is clear that imagination, resourcefulness and creativity are a great advantage when doing church-based evangelism. The possibilities which I have discussed are by no means an exhaustive list of what can be devised and tried. There is so much that churches can do to reach out to their communities in a relevant way. What they need is a willingness to try, and the wisdom to know what will work. If these two things are in place, and evangelistic activities are saturated in prayer, a local church can make real inroads in proclaiming the good news about Jesus.

Discussion Questions

1. What three things would you change about the way your church does evangelism and why?

2. What church based evangelistic programmes has your church run? Discuss how effective they have been and their strengths and weaknesses.

3. What practical steps can your church take to get the most out of their church based evangelistic events?

4. If you could begin with a blank sheet of paper what church based evangelism activities would you initiate?

5. Discuss whether or not there is value in beginning again with a blank sheet and starting afresh. If a particular idea was valuable, would your church be prepared to use it?

CHAPTER 9

Evangelism in the Every Day

I have known James for many years and have always appreciated his abilities as an evangelist. He has such courage and creativity that, when he is with non-Christians, he not only talks about Jesus, but does so in a way that is natural, engaging and challenging. Surprisingly, however, his church has yet to realise what an asset they have. James does not always attend the meetings at church. The communion service is one that he almost never misses, but the family service is one he misses frequently. His argument is that almost no non-Christians come to the family service, so he spends the time mixing with his non-Christian friends. This is true. Often at midday on a Sunday, James is having lunch with a couple of people and he is sharing his faith with them. When the sun is shining, he goes to the local park, where lots of families hang out, and he gets to know people there too, and uses the opportunity to share his faith. Occasionally on a Sunday night, he misses the evening Bible teaching service, though again this is partly because he meets some non-Christian friends in café and there too he witnesses. From James's perspective he is part of the church community and regularly attends communion and the majority of church services, and also helps in the youth club. However, his calling as an evangelist is to be where people are and to share his faith in a natural context. From the perspective of his elders, James has an erratic church attendance record, which shows that he is not a very committed Christian.

Having considered what is involved in church-based evangelism, we now look at what is involved in friendship evangelism, which, as the story above illustrates, is much misunderstood as a method of evangelism. Friendship evangelism could be defined as individual Christians taking the initiative to share the gospel with their contemporaries. It is a form of evangelism that does not depend on organised church programmes but, rather, involves the informal communication of the gospel by motivated individuals. Some have described this as 'gossiping the gospel'. It is precisely this sort of evangelism that we see so often in the book of Acts. In Acts 8: 4, following the martyrdom of Stephen, the Christians who were living in Jerusalem had to scatter throughout Judea and Samaria, but as they went they shared their faith with anyone who would listen. This was not an organised evangelism strategy as such; it was simply believers taking every opportunity to talk about Jesus.

There is a number of reasons why this kind of evangelism is necessary. First, church-based evangelism presupposes that people who are not Christians will nevertheless come to a church event. Certainly in many cases where Christians have built up a relationship with their non-Christian friends this may well be a possibility. However, the majority of people will not want to come to any event that the church holds. Among the reasons for this is the widely held view that the church is a rather frightening place, full of intolerant people, and its activities are boring and irrelevant. Friendship evangelism, on the other hand, does not require any church-based activities or the use of church premises.

Second, church-based evangelism does not in itself produce many initial contacts. In general, people who come to church-based events already have some kind of relationship with Christians prior to darkening the doors of a church building. They come because their Christian friends have invited them. Leaflet drops and newspaper adverts have a very modest effect on church attendance. The majority of non-Christians who come to a church-based event will have been personally invited. When it comes to friendship evangelism, however, initial contacts are made relatively easily. Christians who are committed to evangelism will make contacts among their friends, neighbours, colleagues and just about anybody they come into contact with.

Third, in order for church-based evangelism to be effective, the people being reached have to be at a certain stage in their spiritual awareness. No matter how user-friendly a church event may be, there will always be a little pensiveness on the part of the person being invited. Unless they are utterly stupid, they will be aware that this church wants them to convert, and this is a pressure, even if it is something they want to do. Friendship evangelism can happen even if the person is nowhere spiritually and has no inclination to become a Christian. The person is not being pressurised. They are simply hearing, in an informal setting, that God loves them and can make a difference in their lives.

Finally, church-based evangelism requires infrastructure. In order for it to happen, you need facilities, people, organisation and more often than not a budget. Friendship evangelism requires none of these things. It does not need context, location, planning or finance. It just needs Christians who are friendly and can talk about Jesus.

Though the two types of evangelism are quite different, they are nonetheless complementary. As Christians make contacts with people who are unchurched, they can develop their relationships to the point where they can involve their new-found friends with some church-based activities. In this way, they can get support from other church members to communicate something of the gospel. Friendship evangelism can therefore be seen as a feeder into church-based evangelism.

Some dangers

Though it is a crucial plank in a church's evangelism strategy, it must be noted that there are some inherent dangers in friendship evangelism. These need not be a problem, if we are aware of them and are therefore prepared. The first danger is linked with the fact that to be effective in friendship evangelism, Christians need to make friends with non-Christians and spend time with them. Their positive influence within that circle of people is part of what it means to be salt and light. This relationship-building with people who are not Christians can sometimes result in difficult questions having to be asked. Do I go to the pub with my friends? What should I do when I am asked to go out clubbing? How should I behave when I am in a friend's house and he begins smoking dope? What should my response be if I drop in for a visit to my friend's house for the evening and he is watching pornography? Should I accept the invitation to go away for the weekend with my friend who will be sharing a room with his gay partner? Should I attend my gay friend's wedding to his gay partner? These are not hypothetical questions, but rather real ones that will impact us if we are genuinely involved in our community and in the lives of people in the community.

These questions are not always easy to answer. Nowhere in the Bible are we told not to go into pubs or some of the other places we might venture. That does not necessarily mean that it is permissible, or helpful, but the decision to go or not should be thought about carefully. We need to think about what we are able to handle spiritually, what this will do for the relationship we have with people and the impact it could have on our testimony. This is one of those situations where we need to be wise as serpents yet gentle as doves. However, we do need to realise that if we cut ourselves off from people we will not be able to get alongside them to witness.

This relationship-building with non-Christians should not crowd-out Christians spending time with other Christians. It is also important that Christians do not go out of their depth when engaging in friendship evangelism. It would be tragic if anyone became so immersed in a non-Christian atmosphere that they became absorbed into it. That would not lead to more converts, but rather to fewer committed Christians.

Another danger linked with friendship evangelism is that a Christian could be positively influencing his friends to think about Christianity, but with no reference to the church. This is dangerous because it could ultimately lead to these contacts thinking that Christianity and church are two different things. I have heard many people say to me, 'You can be religious without going to church'. In our postmodern society many want to enjoy their own private spirituality without having the accountability of being part of a local church. We must never give people this excuse. While it might not be wise to invite friends to church activities after the first conversation about spiritual matters, the church must at some time come into the dialogue. Otherwise there will be conversions but no church growth.

A third danger that can arise is that Christians who are involved in friendship evangelism can develop very claustrophobic relationships with those they witness to. I have sometimes seen Christians bring others to a point of decision and develop such a close relationship with the people they are witnessing to that they become followers of those who lead them to Christ as well as followers of Christ himself. The Christian can also seek to prevent the convert from developing a relationship with a church because he or she thinks that no one else can be trusted with the task of nurture, or because of fears that the church is not convert-friendly (some are not, and the leaders need to do something about it!). Our priority in evangelism is to focus people's minds on Christ and encourage them to be loyal to him, not to us. We should not be in the business of evangelism to meet our own emotional needs. It is a task that must be performed selflessly and with humility. And new converts should be integrated into a suitable church as soon practicable after conversion.

The difficulties

As well as these inherent dangers, there are also some more practical difficulties that we need to address as we get involved in friendship evangelism. First and foremost is the fact that most Christians have very few non-Christian friends. Each year at Tilsley College, I begin my evangelism classes by asking the students to make a list of their ten closest friends. I then ask them to put an asterisk beside the name of any friend on this list who is not a Christian. The results are often very revealing. The majority of students only have two or three friends on the list who are not Christians. There is also a link between the length of time a person has been a Christian and the number of non-Christian friends, with new Christians having more non-Christian friends. Though some students are better than others at making friends with non-Christians, and generally speaking young Christians today are better at doing this than young Christians were twenty years ago, only a few of my students have a large number of close friends who are non-Christian.

It is worth noting that all of the students in our college are committed Christians and many go on to the mission field and plant churches around the world. Nevertheless, despite their commitment to evangelism and the extending of God's kingdom, few are good at befriending people who are not Christians. One interesting twist is that, while students are better now at friendship evangelism than they were twenty years ago, they don't know their Bibles as well as students did twenty years ago.

If friendship evangelism is a problem with highly motivated Bible college students, it will be an even bigger problem in the Church at large. As Christians, we have become so withdrawn from the society around us that many of us are simply not in a position to be salt and light. Let me illustrate the problem with a parable.

Mr. Jones has just become a Christian. He is in his early thirties, single, upwardly mobile and has an active social life. Through the witness of some Christians at his place of work, he becomes a Christian and goes to church for the first time. He finds it a strange place, but people are warm and friendly and openly welcome him into their homes. This he enjoys, though his new Christian friends all seem to discourage him from spending too much time with his existing friends. Clearly, they are concerned that his 'old' friends will be a bad influence on him and might drag him back into his former lifestyle. Mr. Jones does not fully understand the logic of the situation, but the combined pressure of these well-intentioned church members, and the teaching in church against worldliness, make it hard for him to do otherwise.

In any case, since going to church and socialising with his new Christian friends, Mr. Jones finds that he has little time to mix with his non-Christian friends anyway. The result is that he sees less and less of them, until he barely regards them as friends at all. In a few short years he has gone from being in touch with a great many non-Christians at work and in his social life to having no non-Christian friends at all. Like most of the Christians in his church, he has effectively cut himself off from the very people who desperately need what he has experienced, namely Jesus Christ.

Though parabolic, this has indeed happened in churches all over the country. It is easy to understand why it happens, but this withdrawing from the world in which we live is neither biblical nor an effective policy. It merely builds into the church a siege mentality that makes it more and more difficult to reach out to a dying world. In the old westerns, there is a familiar scene that is an inherent part of the storyline. A line of wagons is snaking its way across the prairie and being watched by some Indians already covered in their war paint. The Indians attack and the wagons circle for protection. As the Indians swirl around the circle of wagons, the cowboys fire their guns out at them. This could be a good picture of much of our church evangelism. From behind the protective walls of our church, we fire out the gospel, hoping to get some hits. We do not venture out among the noise and confusion, in case we get hurt.

Another problem that many Christians face is that they do not know how to be natural about their Christian faith. Due to the secular nature of our society, they feel that they have to live a double life. There is the spiritual part of their life where they attend church on a Sunday and read their Bibles in the privacy of their homes. Then there is the secular part of their life where they go to work, chat to their neighbours over the garden fence and socialise. These two lives are not integrated, and they rarely meet. Occasionally some Christians get a conscience about this and feel that they really need to say something spiritual to a non-Christian. They pluck up the courage and go for it. However, in their anxiety to say something telling, they shove an indigestible amount of theological information down the throats of their friends and do so with such force that it ends up being counterproductive. Clearly this situation is not good.

A way forward

Having noted both the dangers and the difficulties of friendship evangelism, we need to think of a way forward, in view of its importance and likely effectiveness in comparison with church-based evangelism on its own. Without the use of friendship evangelism, our evangelistic strategy will be limited to things we can do in a church building. This will seriously inhibit future growth. It is crucial therefore that we learn as churches to mobilise members and involve them in friendship evangelism. This is an area where, for two reasons, church leaders must take the lead. First, because, without their input, many church members will not mobilise themselves to get involved in friendship evangelism, and second, because, without this programme being strategically led from the front, there will be little by way of training, co-ordination or support for those who engage in evangelism.

There are various stages in the process of moving people out into friendship evangelism. The first of these is education. The need for education cannot be overstated. It is necessary for two reasons.

First, many Christians have a false view of their role within society. They have misinterpreted Scriptures that talk about Christians being separated from the world. While it is undoubtedly true that we are to have a distinctively Christian lifestyle that will separate us from the sinfulness of the world in which we live, nowhere in the Bible are we told to cut ourselves off and become spiritual hermits within society. Quite the reverse! We are here to be salt and light in society, and that, by its very nature, involves radiating God's light, and acting as a preservative, in our workplace, neighbourhood and among our friends.

It is interesting to note that Jesus was described as the friend of sinners (Mt. 11: 19). Obviously, he led a holy life and modelled godliness to those he rubbed shoulders with. Nevertheless, he did not cut himself off from the crowd, but rather embraced them to the point where his opponents despised him because of the company he kept: mixing with people whose lives were a mess and in moral and spiritual confusion. As Christians get involved at the very heart of society, as they work honourably in their factories, get involved in politics, and play a full role in civic life, so they bring a Christian presence into all of those situations. In that sense, how we go about everyday life is all part of our service to God.

Secondly, education is necessary because many Christians think that evangelism is someone else's responsibility. This is particularly the case if they belong to a church in which there are active evangelists, or the church already has a busy evangelism programme. The average man in the pew thinks that, since evangelism is already happening, he personally does not need to play a role in it. This is not the case, since we are all called to be witnesses whether we like it or not (Acts 1: 8). Each member of the Church is an ambassador, representing God to their friends and neighbours (2 Cor. 5: 20). Somehow, this needs to come through in every church teaching programme.

In my own church, we not only preach frequently on the issue of evangelism: we also find ways of encouraging church members to witness to specific people that they know. One method that we have used is to give each church member a 'covenant card'. On this card there is a space to write the name of a person that they know who is not a Christian. The card asks them to make a commitment to pray for this person, to witness to them and to bring them to a church activity. After prayerful consideration, they sign the card as a declaration before God that they will endeavour to follow the obligations that this demands.

As well as educating church members about their responsibilities in evangelism, we also need to train them to evangelise. A number of things should be included in this training. For example, we need to train people to share their faith in an intelligible way, free from religious jargon, and succinctly. It is also very useful to train people to give their 'testimony', that is to share their personal experience of how God has changed their lives.

In addition, we may need to give some training on how to get in touch with people who are non-Christians and how to share the Christian faith in a non-threatening way. Back in chapter six, I mentioned the fact that in Athens Paul went out to the marketplace to share the gospel. We need to ask what our marketplace is. In essence, it could be any situation where Christians are brought together with non-Christians in a natural setting.

Most Christians already have a marketplace without realising it. Neighbours, colleagues at work and family members are all part of it. We need to train our church members to make the most of opportunities that arise in conversation with these people, and to share the gospel naturally where appropriate. But we can also create new marketplaces. In a society where leisure is so highly prized, there are many opportunities to get alongside people to share the gospel. We can encourage church members to join a chess club, a football team, or the local women's guild, volunteer in a charity shop or begin a book club in their home. All these openings will allow a Christian influence to be felt in many lives and will provide the Christians involved with the opportunity to say something about their faith.

The next stage is to resource the people that have been mobilised for evangelism. This resourcing can take several forms. There are material resources like tracts, Christian books, videos and Bibles. These will prove very useful in the appropriate situations. One friend of mine was witnessing to a man who had many questions about the reliability of the Bible and the truthfulness of Christianity. He was able to give the man a copy of the book *Evidence that Demands a Verdict* by Josh McDowell. It proved to be hugely helpful and the man eventually became a Christian. I have also used and recommended everything from DVDs on apologetics, useful web sites and apps that communicate the gospel and inform Christians, to booklets on bereavement. These resources, if used widely, can be very powerful indeed.

Another form of resourcing that often gets overlooked is that of spiritual support, which includes both advice and prayer. I have already mentioned the fact that Christians can find themselves in difficult situations, as they become involved in the lives of those to whom they are witnessing. Friendship evangelism makes us vulnerable to temptation and spiritual attack. Soldiers on the frontline of a battle suffer a high casualty rate. The spiritual battle that rages when Christians carry the gospel with them is no less real. Unless we learn to support them and provide them with spiritual back-up, they will suffer.

It is important that all the evangelism that is being done is coordinated. There is a sense in which the level of coordination will be dependent on the stage reached and the level of interest being shown. For example, it would be neither feasible nor desirable to coordinate all the many conversations that take place between church members and their non-Christian friends. However, if some of those non-Christians were beginning to show real interest and were asking meaningful questions about the Christian faith, then some measure of coordination would be possible. It might involve the following:

1. Those involved in evangelism could share with members of the church the names of contacts so that others can pray for them. This could be done informally or in a house group or prayer meeting. One church that I visit in Korea keeps an on-going list of contacts which is updated weekly and published in the church bulletin for prayer.
2. Leaders could keep in touch with people who are actively involved in friendship evangelism, and offer advice and pastoral care.
3. Other church members could be introduced to the contacts in an informal setting so that they too could be a positive influence. Recently a group of people from our church went to the cinema. Several of the group brought non-Christian contacts with them, and in this context

we were able to get to know those people in a relaxed environment, which was a help to those who had made the initial contact. If other church members invite the person involved in evangelism and their contact to a meal, that can be of similar benefit.

4. Small prayer groups or prayer triplets could be set up to pray specifically and regularly for contacts.

One final issue that needs to be thought about is how to introduce the person being contacted to the life of the church. It seems to me that a church that is committed to friendship evangelism will also have to put on regular, user-friendly events to which church members can bring their contacts. Bearing in mind that these occasions might be the very first time that the contact has ever been to any kind of church event, they need to be thought through very carefully. The kind of all-age services or one-off events mentioned in the previous chapter would be ideal.

It is said that first impressions last. To a degree I think this is true. The first experience of a church event will colour the way a non-Christian perceives church. This first meeting must be planned. The responsibility for this lies both with the person who has made the contact and the leadership of the church. The person who has made the contact needs to communicate well with the leadership of the church so that there will be awareness about who is coming to the event. It is also the responsibility of this person to decide what kind of event their friend would be best suited to. Some questions might need to be asked. Is my friend very sceptical about Christianity? Does he find it difficult to mingle in big crowds? Would a more subtle approach be appropriate or is he at the stage where he needs to be challenged about his spiritual condition in an up-front way? These questions will help to determine how the contact should be introduced to the church.

The leaders of the church also have a role to play. They need to ensure that there is a range of events that people could be brought to in the first place. These events could vary from something as unthreatening as a barbeque or family fun-day to something more direct like an evangelistic service. They should also ensure that there will be a warm welcome for visitors. This needs to be stated, because it does not always happen. I have often gone into strange churches while on holiday and had the uncomfortable experience of not being welcomed by anyone. Some churches are naturally friendly and have people who find it easy and natural to chat to newcomers, but others do not. In the Bellshill culture, where my church is situated, it would not be a natural thing to walk up to a complete stranger and welcome them. It takes a special kind of person to do this. Church leaders need to ensure that such people are available and ready to do their job. It is helpful to have an actual welcoming team, whose job is to befriend people and chat to them as they come into the event. The welcome team have a vital role to play, because they only have about 30 seconds to get it right. This does not necessarily mean a group of people standing at the church door ready to pounce on people as soon as they walk in. But there must be a structure in place that ensures that every visitor feels at home and cared for.

Discussion Questions

1. What are the advantages and dangers of friendship evangelism?
2. What might prevent people in your church engaging in friendship evangelism and how do we overcome this?
3. How do we get the balance between involvement in the life of the church and involvement in the community and what principles should safeguard this balance?
4. What should we do to introduce unchurched people to the life of the church?

CHAPTER 10

Thinking Mission

There are times in life when different worlds seem to collide. A couple of years ago I was on a trip out to Pakistan. The flight took me via Dubai in the United Arab Emirates. I was due to spend several hours in Dubai airport before getting my connection on to Islamabad. That didn't concern me, as I had often come through Dubai in the past and loved wandering around the huge airport terminal, with all its colour and bustle.

As I sat in the airport terminal sipping a latte, I noted that the TV in the bar was advertising the Palm Jumeirah. This is a man-made archipelago, which juts out from the Dubai coast in the shape of a palm and has been dubbed the eighth wonder of the world. On the giant palm are built thousands of homes, dozens of hotels and even the palm's own monorail. The advert showed how this multi-billion dollar project came together with awe-inspiring precision, as 40,000 construction workers laboured to make it a reality.

Having left Dubai, I went on to Islamabad and then headed north by road to a school I was visiting. The school was having an extension built, and I thought I would take a look. The budget for the school's extension was only a fraction of that of the Palm Jumeirah. However, that was not the only difference. The foreman of the school project did not give the impression that he knew what he was doing. There was a complete lack of coordination in the management of the project, and the small team of builders spent more time standing around talking than they did building. As these two worlds collided in my head, I could graphically see what a difference it makes to a project when it operates according to a planned strategy.

Planning an evangelistic strategy

Whether the emphasis of a church's evangelism is focused on church-based evangelism, personal evangelism or both, there is need for an overall strategy. All too often, churches go about their evangelism in a random way, without carefully planning how they will reach others. Often this is because the gifted evangelists within the church, many of whom will be very spontaneous people, are just left to get on with it. As they also tend to be individualists, they do not mind this. So they will be inclined to do what comes naturally, but will not necessarily take the time to think about the big picture and ask questions about the church's overall evangelism strategy. If a church is full of enthusiastic evangelists, then there will be an impact, but the effect could be greatly enhanced by careful planning.

But how does a church go about developing a coherent strategy for evangelism? The answer is to do it carefully, methodically and in stages. This is a long-term issue, not something that will be resolved in just a few weeks. The task of making disciples is such an important one that no amount of time and effort is too much. We need to work out a strategy that will be effective, and also maintain that effectiveness by continuing to respond to needs that we see around us.

Analysis

The first stage in the process of developing a strategy is to ask the question, Where are we now? It is self-evident that if we want to get anywhere, we need to know what our starting point is. I do a lot of driving because of my job, and often drive to places I have never been to before. A few years ago, I bought myself a portable satnav, which attaches neatly to the inside of my windscreen and this has greatly helped me to get to where I want to go. However, I have discovered an important fact about satnav systems. When you first switch them on, there is a short delay. This is because the satnav is trying to work out its present position. It cannot work out a route to a final destination until it knows where the journey is starting from. The same is true of a church's evangelism strategy. You cannot work out where you want to go unless you know where you are now. Working out where you are now requires analysis.

Analysis is often a very difficult thing, for several reasons. First, it is painful. Any honest analysis will reveal flaws and shortcomings in our evangelism, and most of us don't like admitting to them. Church leaders, in particular, struggle with this because they often think that a lack of effectiveness in the evangelistic work of their church is a personal reflection on their leadership skills. Though to a degree this might be true, two things must be borne in mind. We need to recognise that all of us are fallible humans and that mistakes and shortcomings are part of life. Recognising this is not tantamount to admitting failure or an excuse for mediocrity; it is merely a recognition that even very good leaders need to work hard at what they do, and that every church can do better. We also need to realize that the salvation of lost men and women is incomparably more important than a bruised ego.

If this process of analysis is to be successful, it must be characterised by rigour, honesty and genuinely penetrating questions. There should be no room for flattery, self-congratulation or excuse. The whole point of an analysis is to discover what is working, what is not working at present, and what will never work. There will be two dangers to look out for. First, there is the danger of sacred cows. By that, I mean evangelistic activities to which we have an emotional attachment, but which are ineffective. Second, there is the danger of bypassing successful evangelistic activities, without asking whether this activity can be made more successful. If you can avoid these two pitfalls, then your analysis is much more liable to be useful.

What sort of questions do we need to ask in this analysis? It seems to me that there are two types of question.

The first type seeks to assess the general spiritual health of the church. Though these questions are not specifically related to evangelism, they are important because churches that are spiritually healthy are more likely to be successful in their evangelism; likewise, churches that are lifeless, where the members lack passion and a love for God, are likely to be unsuccessful in reaching others for Christ.

The following are examples of this type of question:

- Is this church deeply committed to the Bible?
- Are the members of this church committed to prayer?
- Is this church unified?
- Does this church have a unified vision?
- Do these church members have a passion for worship?
- To what extent is this church concerned with the glory of God?
- Are the members of this church determined to work hard for the church?
- Are church members committed to holiness and sacrificial service?

Each of these questions must be answered honestly. The answers will indicate whether we are genuinely ready to grow as a church or not. We may get people coming along to our church services, but that is not necessarily growth. Real growth involves people committing themselves to Jesus Christ, and then developing in their spiritual maturity. Remember we are disciple-makers, not scalp-hunters.

The second type of question assesses whether the evangelism being done by the church is effective. It goes further and seeks to determine if our churches are geared up for the specific task of evangelism and disciple making. The following are examples of the kind of question that we need to be asking:

- How successful is this church in reaching out to unchurched people?
- Is this church prepared to be innovative in its outreach?
- How welcome do strangers feel when they come to church?
- How loved and cared for do church members feel?
- To what extent are the members of this church mobilized for action?
- Does this church have the gifting available for innovative evangelism?
- Are we as a church aware of the spiritual needs of the community?
- What are we prepared to do to meet those needs?

Without being too harsh, I would want to suggest that if your church has a 'low score' on each of these questions, then it is simply not ready to make disciples. A divided, unfriendly, tradition-bound and unwilling church will not be an effective one.

When this analysis has been done, it is important to avoid the twin evils of complacency and negativity. If your church scores highly on these questions, it is easy to feel that things are sufficiently good and rest on your laurels. This is deadly! No matter how well your church is doing, it could always be doing better. It is also possible that at some time in the future your church will be doing less well. There is a fine balance between an active church which is growing and a church which is beginning to slow down and lose momentum. Slowdown and decline often happens so gradually, it can go unnoticed. It begins with the church flat-lining, that is, the church just takes its foot off the pedal and loses a sense of forward momentum. Initially, nothing seems to be wrong; there is just no actual growth. In my experience, once a church begins to plateau in this way, it has about eighteen months to change before real decline sets in. By this time, church members have become so used to inertia that the church is actually in real trouble. We need to bear in mind that churches lose people through natural wastage. People grow old and die; others leave because their careers take them elsewhere. Because of this wastage, unless new people are joining, the church will decline. The lesson is clear: even if the church appears healthy, vigilance is never out of place.

If your church does rather badly in relation to these questions, you need to avoid despairing. The situation is indeed gloomy, but it can change if there is a will to bring about change. A church is beaten only if its members want to be beaten. With prayer and concerted effort, it is possible to turn a church around. I know of one church near my home that reversed serious decline. The church had shrunk to just nine members, all of whom were pensioners. The one remaining elder asked a couple from a nearby church to come and help. They agreed to do so, but only on the proviso that this one elder would step down and give them complete freedom to do whatever it would take to bring about growth. The elder graciously did so, and today the church numbers a hundred and fifty. There is always hope where there is a will. The key is to go through the pain of honest assessment and to change. Be positive and focus, not on where your church is now, but on where it could be. Seeing potential and tapping it is one of the secrets of church growth.

Setting goals

Once the analysis is complete, the next stage is to begin setting goals. It is one thing to discover where you are at present; it is quite another to decide where you want to go. There is an old adage that says, 'If you aim at nothing, you are bound to get there.' This is quite true when it comes to setting church goals. Unless you determine what you want your church to be like, you will not have any direction to go in. This listless drift will never lead to people becoming Christians and the church growing.

Not only is it important to set goals, you need to set the right kind of goals. This requires careful thought. Too much haste, and your church could end up running hard in the wrong direction. But if the goals you set are the right ones, you can move forward in a united and confident way. Whatever goals you set, they should have the following characteristics:

They should be realistic.

This sounds obvious, but it is easy to allow enthusiasm to get the better of you and to rush into aiming for goals which you will never be able to achieve. Remember that you might be limited by a lack of personnel, gifting and even finance, so realism is important. Goals that are not realistic will eventually lead to discouragement when they are not reached. Better to set goals that are reachable and to have the satisfaction of being able to say, 'With God's help we did it.'

By definition, realistic goals are neither overly pessimistic not hugely optimistic. The balance needs to be somewhere in the middle. For my own church, that has a membership of forty-five, it would be just as mistaken to set a goal of one new member over the next five years as to expect five hundred. Your goal-setting will require both sanctified common sense and belief in the power of God. You may also want to have some interim goals, or goals that are set in stages. This way, you can make progress and still be pressing on in the right direction. It also makes it possible to include goals that your church is not presently capable of reaching, but will be at some time in the future.

They should be measurable

Again this sounds obvious, but in my experience it is easy to set goals without asking the question, 'How will we know when we have got there?' Goals need to be measurable, so that you know when you have crossed over the line and made those goals part of history. It is very encouraging to look back and see in concrete terms what has been achieved.

Part of the measurement process is having a timescale. Like the goals themselves, the timescale needs to be realistic. Some goals might be achieved fairly quickly, while others take some time and will need to be part of a rolling programme. Be careful not to have timescales that demand progress too soon. Some things will take time to achieve and should not be rushed, so patience is necessary. On the other hand, don't get used to the luxury of allowing too much time, or the sense of urgency will be lost.

Measurable goals demand specific targets. If you say that your goal is to do more outreach, that is open to a great deal of subjective interpretation. It is altogether too vague. It would be better to have the goal of presenting the gospel to one hundred people over the next year, or to increase church membership by five people over the next two years. These goals can be measured in terms of quantity and timescale. Measurable goals lead to specific achievements, and they give a focus to our efforts.

They should be visionary

It is important when setting goals not to underestimate the potential that your church has when being used by an almighty God. A friend of mine once said that you should fill church committees with optimists. I believe this to be at least partly true. Certainly the people at the forefront of your church should be visionaries and people of real faith. We have a great God and one who can work powerfully through failing individuals like us. We need to get an insight into God's vision for our community, and set goals accordingly.

They should be prayerful

Goals should also be prayerfully set. As an elder in a church, I constantly need to remind myself that the church I help to lead is God's church, not mine. In setting goals for our church, we always need to recognise that God's will is paramount. This is not an excuse for fatalistic inactivity. Rather we need to seek God's direction at all times and move forward listening to his voice. Anyone who has been in ministry for any length of time will also know that ultimately we are powerless, as we are dealing with spiritual realities. God is the one who challenges hearts and changes lives. Following his leading and fitting into his plans is therefore the only way to go. He has given us minds to think and plan, and we must use these, but we must never leave God out of our decision making process; rather we should always be listening for his prompting.

They should be agreed

One final point that needs to be made is that the goals that are set for a particular church should have the consent of the members of that church. Better still, the members need to own the vision. Many leaders are very good at creating ideas and strategies for evangelism, but very poor at bringing the rest of the church along with them. Practicalities dictate that the goals of a church will be decided on by a few, but they should be communicated to the church as a whole and sold in such a way that the church members get excited about them. If the whole church can agree to the goals, the battle is half won. Make time to talk to church members and keep them up to speed with what is happening. This is time well spent, and keeps the whole church engaged in the vision-casting process.

Determining methods

Once you have set your goals, the next stage is to decide how those goals can be accomplished. Often churches can be activity-based and feel that they are doing their job because a lot of things are happening. This is not necessarily the case. In fact, indulging in excessive activity can be counterproductive. Having lots of activities and then trying to find a rationale for them is a bit like putting the cart before the horse. It is much better to decide what you want to achieve (by setting goals) and then try to find ways of achieving it. Creating an unwieldy monster of activity that is hard to maintain and directionless will not make the most of the resources that your church possesses. It is also often very difficult to bring an activity to an end once you have started it. Don't create monsters, create well-oiled machines. Make sure that the activities you create are actually the ones you need.

The time will inevitably come when you have to slaughter the sacred cows that I mentioned earlier. There are always some activities that simply do not work and so need to be ditched. No church will have enough people to sustain them: they are an unnecessary luxury. The problem is that some of the people involved in these activities will have an emotional attachment to them. This is partly because they have good memories of the days when they did work and partly because they simply enjoy them.

I can remember a youth club that we used to run in my church. It was a lot of fun and most of the leaders enjoyed it, despite the rowdiness of the kids. As the years went by, however, there seemed to be nothing to show for all our work. The youth club did give us credibility in the community and made our church known, but no young people were becoming Christians. Ultimately we had to make changes. The club had served its purpose in establishing contacts with people in the locality, but our new goal was to see young people trust Christ, and the old method was simply not delivering this. It was hard to see the club go, but we began a new one with a new format that was much better suited to the goals that we had set. Be merciless with the sacred cows and the dividends will rapidly become apparent.

As you set about determining the methods that will achieve your goals, there is a number of questions you need to ask. They are simple, but they will determine whether or not your methods are appropriate.

Can the church wear the method?

When it comes to the issue of determining methods, it is necessary to be pragmatic and ask if the members of your church will be willing to see this method being used. After all, evangelism and disciple-making is the job of the whole church, not just a few specialists. The more people in your church get involved, the more likely you are to make a real impact. You are therefore reliant upon the support of church members.

Sometimes when it comes to new initiatives, people need a little coaxing. Human beings enjoy routine and therefore need to be convinced that something different is really worthwhile. Often church leaders will be able to sell ideas to their congregation, but not always. It is here that good judgment is necessary. You need to decide if you should push ahead with a particular method, even though some people in the church will be very unhappy, or if the price is too high to pay. Alternatively, you can wait and educate, in the hope that in time this is a method you will be able to use without too much resistance. However, if the method will simply never be accepted by members of your church, perhaps it is better to move on to another method.

Do we have the manpower?

A second practical concern is whether or not you have the people to carry out the proposed method. I have come across many good evangelistic ideas in my travels that require a lot of people to carry them out. In a small church where people are already busy, some of the ideas you might have for evangelism might just be too much for the limited personnel.

Do we have the gift?

Even when you have enough people to carry out some evangelistic activity, you still need to ask if you have the right kind of people, or rather the right kind of gifts. Again, I have come across many innovative forms of outreach, but they require a special kind of gifting. They may be very effective, but only if you have the right kind of people who can carry them out.

Will this method achieve the goals?

This question takes us right back to our goals (which is where we want to be). With every idea that you can think about, you will need to continually refer back to the goals you have set and ask if this method will really work. If not, then don't even think of using it. You will merely be building up your stock of sacred cows, just when you want to be depleting it!

Is this the best method?

Even when you come across an idea that is likely to work, you still need to ask if it is the best possible method. This will, of course, send you back to the drawing board; but why design something that will have mediocre success, when you can have something that will be very successful?

It is important to remember that the right method will always achieve more than the wrong one, so it pays to take the time to get it right. At this point, it must be stated that coming up with good methods for reaching people will require a great deal of imagination and creativity. The job of leadership is to lead, but not all leaders will be creative individuals. It is essential that the most creative people in your church are encouraged to come up with methods and initiatives. A lack of creativity is one of my weaknesses. I have no problem talking to people about my faith. To this extent, I do believe that I have been given the gift of evangelism: I can communicate my faith coherently and can back up my claims with convincing arguments. But when it comes to dreaming up new ideas for evangelism or finding ways of getting into the community, I am not very good. Thankfully there are people in my church who are good at doing this and, as a team, we can be effective. The lesson is clear. We need to use all the gifts that God has given us, and together we will be able to make an impact. There is also real value in looking at what other churches do. I preach at lots of churches both in the UK and abroad. I frequently pick up ideas that we can use in my church. This cross-fertilisation is a great benefit, so it is good to meet up with people from other churches and see what ideas will be transferrable.

Implementation

Even when you have come up with a series of methods that will achieve your stated goals, the job is still not done. You now have to implement those methods. In my experience, this is the most difficult stage in the whole process. It is one thing to excite people in your church with a series of goals and come up with the right methodology; it is quite another to get people doing something. The triple evils of laziness, apathy and fear will conspire against you. The Bible pictures the church as an army ready for battle (Eph. 6: 10–20), but sometimes local churches are no more than a collection of mavericks and deserters. Getting action out of the 'slumbering saints' and unity among the lone rangers is a tricky job indeed. It will take significant leadership skill to get everyone working together.

But implementing methods is more complex than just rousing the troops. If the methods you are proposing are very different than those already in place, then any progress may involve wholesale change. The existing structures may prove inadequate, and entirely new structures may need to be put in place.

Let me give one simple example. About thirty years ago, many independent evangelical churches decided that the Sunday evening evangelistic service was not producing the goods. The main reason for this was that most of the people that these services targeted were in their homes watching primetime TV. Many of these churches then decided to introduce a morning all-age service. This was to be the new method of reaching people. The problem was that the church 'worship service' was held in the morning and there was therefore a clash in the programme. In order to facilitate this method, the Sunday programme had to be changed. Some churches did this by moving the worship service to an earlier slot while others moved it to the evening. The reality is that this move split some churches, though the end result was undoubtedly for the best. This is the kind of change that new methods necessitate.

Change is never easy, and many churches do not manage change well. Despite this the effort must be made. Without a willingness to change inadequate structures and bring in new ones, the new methods will never make the journey from the drawing board to reality. As you go about restructuring, the need for rationalisation may become apparent. No one church can do everything. However big and talent-laden a church may be, it will always have its limitations. As new structures and methods are put into practice, adding to the overall burdens of the church, something will have to go. You need to ask yourself what the priorities are. A particular activity may be perfectly valid and effective, but if the resources (human and otherwise) are simply not available, then it cannot happen. It is better to do a smaller number of things well than to do more, but do them badly.

Here are a few things that will prove useful when it comes to implementing change. They may prove to make the difference between new methods failing or succeeding.

Move towards every-member ministry.

If the teaching of the New Testament is to be taken seriously, then we must recognise that every person within a church has something to contribute to the life of the church (1 Cor. 12: 12–30). Not everyone in your church will be able to preach, come up with creative ideas or demonstrate leadership ability, but they will all have some gift to offer. Without doubt, the greatest resource that any church has is its membership, its people. The problem is that, in most churches, the 20/80 rule applies. That is, 20% of the church members do 80% of the work. This means that most of the gifting in the church lies dormant. This problem is partly caused by the fact that in every church there are people who are simply not willing to pull their weight. However, leadership can also be a problem. Some church leaders are not good at identifying gift or ensuring that each person in the church has a role. Laziness in church life has to be challenged—it is a sin. Leaders also need to be aware of what members are capable of, and motivate them into action.

Jesus told Peter to feed his sheep (John 21: 15–17). The analogy of sheep is a good one when it comes to church members, because both need to be guided. It is the responsibility of the leaders in a church to guide members of a church into roles that they can fulfil. The more people that are involved in the methods that you have devised, the more likely those methods are to succeed.

Identify key people

As well as promoting every-member involvement, it is also important to identify key people to spearhead the work. With the best will in the world, not every member of the church will be able to head up a particular work or provide the vision and driving force necessary to carry it through. Enthusiasm is great, but it does not achieve the same as real ability. There needs to be a core of capable and enthusiastic people who can carry the burden of an activity and ensure that it is done well. Part of the art of leadership is to find these people. I often talk about looking for game-changing people who can be given a game-changing agenda. In other words, people who have the ability to really make things happen and can be given real responsibility to carry things forward.

Identify these key people and delegate enough responsibility to them, so that they have a fulfilling and demanding brief. Sometimes, doing this can be met with protest, because churches often prize teamwork. I am committed to teamwork as well. However, the two things are complementary. Teams within a church can be led and motivated by these key people. They will give a team its drive and momentum. Real teamwork does not quash entrepreneurship or leadership. Rather a good team will allow the entrepreneur and the leader to do their job, and will offer them the support they need to make things happen. There is nothing as powerful as assembling the 'movers and shakers' in your congregation and unleashing them into a particular task. Provided they are spiritual people who have correct motives and are accountable to the leadership of the church and willing to work with others, they will be a potent force. Ultimately it is these key people who will really make things happen as far as outreach is concerned. Mobilize them and the results will follow.

Break stereotypes

One of the traps that will snarl up progress is a fear of setting a precedent. Often church members will say, "We never did that before". It is true that if you are developing new structures to accommodate your methods, you will be doing things that you never did before. This is not a negative thing; it is positive provided that change leads to greater effectiveness. Change for change's sake is never a good idea, but change that makes a church more effective is. Church members need to be educated to embrace change and thrive with it.

Ensure that your thinking doesn't become calcified or dominated by stereotypes. The New Testament does have a few things to say about church structure, but not many. There is no one prescribed way of structuring church life and the early church encompassed great variety. Erickson comments that 'the only didactic passages on church government are Paul's enumerations of the basic qualifications for offices'[1] Individual churches in the New Testament were free to structure themselves in a way that was relevant to their own situation, and so are we. New Testament Christianity was fluid, creative, passionate, inventive, relational and able to mould itself into any cultural setting. To be truly New Testament, today's churches need to be like this. Be willing to break the stereotypes, and don't feel that you need to copy anyone else. Each church must do what is appropriate in its own situation.

---

1   Millard J. Erickson, *Christian Theology*, Ada MI: Baker Publishing, revised edition 2013, p. 1094.

Be courageous

It is important in this whole process to be courageous. Have the courage to try something new and to stand by your decisions even if, initially, they are not universally popular. Very few things can be achieved in a church without courage.

Evaluation

The final stage in the process of developing a strategy is to have a rigorous evaluation. However much thought you might have put into the preceding stages, you will not necessarily get it right the first time round. We are all fallible, and to err is human. Being able to forgive yourself for mistakes and move on is an important skill to master. What is more, our communities change so very quickly that some of our methods are almost bound to fail or be less effective than you initially envisaged. This is not a problem if your process is flexible in the first place. If at first you don't succeed, then try and try again.

A good evaluation will depend on honest critical thinking. But it requires more than that. You need to be positive as well, and believe that the right solution will be found in time. The problem with trial and error is that people can easily become disillusioned. This must be guarded against, and it is at this stage that the true qualities of leadership shine through. Visionary leaders are able to absorb disappointment, remain enthusiastic and be willing to reinvent or reshape a method so that it will be more effective. This will demand perseverance and a willingness to keep thinking, but, as the alternative is a lack of progress, it is certainly worthwhile.

As you evaluate the work that has been done, two things will help keep you on the right track. First, keep your original goals at the back of your mind. Sometimes in the process of developing a strategy, you can lose sight of your goals. A church can become so wrapped up in the minutiae of detail that its vision fades and the forest cannot be seen for the trees. The goals you have set will be the constraints that prevent any derailing. If you remind yourself of them continually, you may fail to reach them at any one point, but you will have been going in the right direction.

Second, you will need to learn from your ongoing work. Even if a method fails to deliver, all is not lost. Valuable lessons will have been learned which, if utilised, will enable your church to do a better job the next time around. An old expression states: 'History teaches us that history teaches us nothing at all'. There might be a grain of truth in this, but only because people are not willing to learn from their mistakes. If lessons are learned, then, inevitably, you will be in a better position to deal with a similar situation in a better way.

Discussion Questions

1. Analyse the effectiveness of your church is reaching out to un-churched people
2. What goals should you set for your church and why?
3. How would you go about achieving these goals?
4. Think of ways in which you could mobilise people in your church for evangelism?

CHAPTER 11
Sandwich Boards and Megaphones

I was on a plane to Islamabad some time ago, going to preach at a conference there. Sitting in the Boeing 777 next to me was a dapper little Asian man and his slightly less well-dressed wife. They were a pleasant couple and we had a good conversation, ranging from the recession to cultural difference between Europeans and Pakistanis. Eventually he asked me about the reason for my trip, and so I told him, holding up my Bible and mentioning some of the passages I would be preaching from. This led to an extended conversation about faith. It turned out that, while he was of Pakistani origin, he actually lived in Manchester, where he had come across a number of Christians. He was not hostile to Christianity; indeed he liked and was impressed with some of the Christians he had come across. However, he did have some concerns about the differences between Christianity and Islam, in particular the issue of the bodily resurrection of Jesus, as that is something Muslims do not believe in. This then became the centre of our discussions.

Needed answers for new questions

Inevitably, as we move out into the market-place to share the gospel with people, we will be confronted with a great deal of scepticism. I have rarely come across anyone who, at our first meeting, wanted to commit themselves to the Christian faith. More usually, I meet people who are either confused and don't know what to believe, or that believe something very different.

Unless we take the time to deal with the confusion and clear up questions that they have, we will make little progress.

When Peter wrote his first epistle, he commanded the believers to be prepared to give an answer for the hope they had (1 Pet. 3: 15). The word that Peter uses here is *apologia,* which was a legal term used in courtrooms when an argument is given on behalf of a client. What Peter is telling us is that we need as Christians to contend for the faith when we come up against competing worldviews. Apologetics is the weapon we use when dealing with the many questions that we will face. As people express their doubts, we need to be ready to answer them honestly, boldly and with humility—as Peter said, 'with gentleness and respect, keeping a clear conscience so that those who speak maliciously against your good behaviour in Christ may be ashamed of their slander' (1 Pet. 3: 15, 16).It is worth noting in passing that Peter was not some erudite philosopher or academic serving in an elite university. He was a humble fisherman who was nevertheless aware that many worldviews existed in his day. Apologetics is not something that should be reserved for the avid readers or intellectuals among us. It is the responsibility of every Christian to know how to defend and explain their faith.

As we do this, there are some points that we need to be aware of. First, there may be times when we don't have an answer that will fully satisfy the person we are witnessing to. Some years ago I was doing a mission in Malta. The GLO team I was with was conducting an open-air meeting along the sea front. I noted a woman who seemed interested in what we were saying, so I approached her to share the gospel. She confessed that she had attended church since childhood, but then lost interest and fell away. When I asked her why, she gave an answer that clearly was not the real reason for her decision to leave the church. Gently, I asked further questions to find the real reason. She then told me about a tragedy that removed any belief she had in God. She had a daughter who died, at the age of three, of leukaemia. 'Why did God allow that?' she asked me. I suppose that I could have said that it was all down to original sin, but such an answer would have come across as trite and unsatisfying, and even offensive because she might have thought that I was suggesting that some sin of hers had caused the death of her child. In the end,

I just told her that I didn't know, but I assured her of God's love for her and stated that God knows what it is like to lose a child.

The reality is that, sometimes, we don't know the answer to questions. In such situations we should never pretend that we do. It is better to admit that we don't know the answer, than to give one that achieves nothing. Sometimes, it is good to ask for time to think about it, and then come back to the person. But never let your pride push you into giving an answer that is half-baked.

Another thing we need to be aware of is the fact that we can win an argument, but not win the person; rather, in winning, we can alienate. When we do contend for the faith, the objective is not to browbeat the enquirer into intellectual submission, but to clear up any difficulties they might have that prevent them from believing in God. Answering their questions in an argumentative or belligerent way will only cause further problems and put up more barriers to faith. I have a friend who has debated with sceptics, especially atheists, in a number of university campuses. He is an intellectual giant as well as a kind and gentle man of God. He once told me that his primary aim when debating with someone is not simply to win the argument, but rather to win the person. There have been times when he could really have embarrassed his debating opponent by crushing his argument, but he didn't because that would have been hurtful. His balance between intellectual vigour and gentleness is a good one.

A third point that we need to bear in mind is that our arguments will not always be neatly packaged and tied up. Christianity is not something that can be proved scientifically. You will never be able to totally convince a sceptic that it is idiotic and blind not to accept what you believe in. What we can do, however, is to show that a person does not have to commit intellectual suicide in order to become a Christian, and that Christianity is a coherent faith that provides some answers to life's deepest questions. It is the best explanation for the evidence that we have to hand.

Finally, we need to be aware that we cannot make a person a Christian simply by providing them with good answers to their questions. When all is said and done, it is the Holy Spirit who convicts and draws people to faith in God. But the Holy Spirit uses our arguments to show people that the Christian faith is tenable, and then reveals to them that it is true.

There are, of course, many questions that people are asking today. Too many by far to be dealt with in any one book, let alone in one chapter. What I will do is to mention the kind of questions I most often come across, and then give what I feel are credible answers to those questions.

Why should I bother believing in God?

For many people in our post-modern world, the question is not whether God exists but whether he is relevant. The apathy that many people have towards both religion and God is profound. Many just don't care. As one person said to me, "Stephen, if you want to believe in God that's fine, but don't expect me to believe in him, this is not for me, I just couldn't be bothered." We can, of course, quote all kinds of verses about judgment and hell, but this is rarely effective. In many cases, it is precisely the threats of eternal punishment that have turned them off Christianity in the first place.

I would generally counter this apathy by pointing out that life has no ultimate meaning or value without God and the possibility of immortality. If there is no possibility of immortality, then mankind and the universe as a whole will just fizzle out and become nothing. In the words of William Lane Craig, mankind is therefore nothing more than 'a doomed race in a dying universe'[1]. Questions then need to be asked. Was there any real point to mankind existing in the first place? Would it have made any difference if mankind had never existed? If, like the animals, we exist and then we die, then in qualitative terms our life is no different from that of a dog. Moreover, if there is no God, then mere duration prolongation of existence would not make our life meaningful. To live forever with no possibility of ascending to a higher plane would be ultimately meaningless. There would be no point to it. Only the existence of God and the possibility of knowing him can bring meaning to life.

Life would also have no ultimate value if there was no immortality and no God. If there was no possibility of punishment for the wrongs committed in this life, then what motivation is there for doing good? Why should we refrain from hurting others, if there is no one to answer to in the next life and

---

1 William Lane Craig, *Apologetics: an introduction*, Chicago IL: Moody Publishers 1989, p. 41.

therefore no repercussion to be faced? In any case, if God does not exist, how do we decide what is right and wrong? Crimes like rape and murder cannot be condemned as being wrong. All that we can conclude is that some of us, as individuals, do not like these things to be done. But that is purely subjective opinion. Hitler could not be condemned for gassing six million Jews. We do not like what he did, but that is merely our opinion. Without a God to judge between right and wrong, and to be a yardstick against which all actions moral or otherwise can be judged, there is no way of saying what is right or wrong. Only God can impose values on life.

To sum up, there are two good reasons for not being apathetic about the subject of belief in God. If there is no God, then life is devoid of ultimate meaning and there can be no objective moral values. As human beings we are nothing more than slime that evolved by sheer accident, with no reason or purpose to our existence. We are insignificant people living a meaningless existence. Though this might possibly be the case, it would be an unbearable existence once the consequences of the non-existence of God had sunk in. It would also make the world as a whole unbearable—and is doing so. As Ravi Zacharias commented when summing up the destructive force of atheism in society, 'The infrastructure of our society has become mindless and senseless because the foundation upon which we have built cannot support any other kind of structure'[2]. Mankind therefore desperately needs God, for without God life is absurd. That being the case, apathy towards God is not an option.

But does God exist?

Once the necessity of God is emphasized, I often find people asking if God really exists. Occasionally, it is because they are convinced atheists. However, in the vast majority of cases, it is just because they are not sure that someone as intangible and apparently remote as God does actually exist. This could be termed agnosticism. They are not convinced that there is no God, but are not sure that there is a God.

I generally answer this kind of question in three ways. First, I mention the fact that the origin of the universe requires some kind of explanation. There

2 Ravi Zacharias, *Can Man live without God?*, Nashville TN: W. Publishing Group 1994, p. 63.

needs to be a first cause which itself is uncaused. Of course, many sceptics claim that a major alternative explanation for the existence of the universe is the theory of evolution. This, however, is highly problematic. We need to remember that the theory of evolution is just that—a theory—and one that I personally find unconvincing because of its many shortcomings. However, we also need to recognise that evolutionists trace the stages of evolutionary development to the primitive gases from which everything else is said to have evolved, but they cannot explain the origin of matter or life. They do not have a first cause. They can and do claim that everything began with a big bang that occurred some 13.5 billion years ago, but they cannot explain the cause behind the big bang. In that sense they, too, are taking a step of faith as they hold to their theory. I would also point out that even if evolutionary theory could be proved to be true, that does not prove that God does not exist. Indeed, to make such a statement would be to confuse categories. When we talk about the theory of evolution we are referring to a mechanism; however, this is different from an ultimate explanation. Mechanism and cause should not be confused. God could quite easily have chosen to use evolution as his means of creation: so at best the evolutionist can claim that this is his explanation for how life develops—not an explanation for why life exists, or how matter came into being, in the first place. It is also a theory that is increasingly under siege and in need of re-evaluation.

How then can we explain the origin of the universe? In order for the universe to have come into existence, there must have been something that caused it to exist but which was not itself caused. To use an analogy, if you see a train carriage moving along, and then another and another, it is logical to deduce that at the end of these carriages there is an engine which is pushing them, but which is not itself being pushed. Go back far enough in time, and you must have something or someone who created the universe, but who was not created. Or to put it another way, the universe must depend for its existence on something that is totally independent and uncaused. By definition, this must be God.

A second line of reasoning that I use is to talk about the inherent design and orderliness that appears to be present in the universe. This kind of argumentation was used effectively some two hundred years ago by a Christian philosopher called William Paley. He used the analogy of a watch, something that is very much simpler than the universe. Paley reasoned that if he came across a watch lying on the ground and inspected it, his conclusion, even if he had never seen a watch before, would be that it was something designed by an intelligent being, rather than something that just happened to be there. He would reach this conclusion because the watch had many gears and a spring that worked together to make the hands move in perfect coordination with each other. If we would logically conclude that something as simple as a watch was designed and therefore had to have a designer, then the universe that is infinitely more complex and demonstrates much more sophisticated coordination also has to have a designer.

To suggest that the universe just happened is to stretch the point well beyond credulity. As William Dembski stated, 'undirected natural causes can throw scrabble pieces on a board but cannot arrange the pieces to form meaningful words or sentences'[3.] The odds against the universe being a freak cosmic accident that is uncaused or undirected are infinitesimally small. In order for the universe to contain a life-permitting planet like earth, there are a whole set of constants that must be in place to create the initial conditions upon which the laws of nature operate. These conditions fall into an extraordinary narrow range of life permitting values. If they were altered even slightly, life could not happen. For example, if there was a change in the strength of the atomic weak force by only one part in 10^{100}, then life could not exist.

Likewise, many things within the universe show evidence of complex design. The human eye, for example, cannot be adequately explained without the presence of an intelligent designer. Even a microscopic flagellum with its multiple integrated components requires a design explanation. Design can be seen everywhere and all around us. With each evidence of design, we can rightly declare that there must have been a designer.

A third line that I would choose is to talk about is the innate sense of morality that human beings seem to possess. We do not just react instinctively to situations, but have a sense of what is right, wrong and noble. If the average person in the street were to be asked to comment on the holocaust or the

3 William Dembski (ed.), *Mere Creation: Science, Faith & Intelligent Design,* Downers Grove IL: Inter-Varsity Press 1998, p.15, Introduction (Dembski).

actions of the 9/11 bombers or the Yorkshire Ripper, he would immediately say that these were very evil acts. He may not know the basis on which he makes these moral assertions, but he would instinctively know they were wrong. Again, people do make great personal sacrifices for the benefit of others. This moral sense cannot be explained as mere environmental conditioning, since it occurs in the lives of people from every culture and background, though not necessarily in a uniform way. Neither can noble thoughts and actions find their origin in random evolutionary processes. They can, however, be understood if God exists. For he, as a moral being, can create us with a sense of morality, and this is precisely what the Bible claims.

How do we know the Bible is true?

Even if the people to whom we witness accept that there is a God and that mankind needs God, this position is still a long way from accepting the truth about God that is presented in Scripture. This brings us to the question of how we know the Bible is true. For many people, the Bible is just another religious book, no different from the Koran or the Bhagavad Gita. Why do we as Christians believe that the Bible is the word of God, and why do we believe that the manuscripts that we have today are correct?

I would tend to approach this question in a number of ways. First, I would deal with the philosophical issue of what is true and what is not true. In our post-modern multicultural society, questions are raised about whether absolute truth exists. Everyone has their own truth and no one truth can claim supremacy over another. The problem arises, however, when two truth claims prove to be mutually contradictory. For example, some people might claim that Christians, Muslims and Hindus all worship the same God. But when you look at how the respective scriptures of these world religions describe the nature and character of God, the various accounts contradict each other. For the Christian, God is a Trinity, for the Muslim, God is one, and for the Hindu, there are many gods. Such contradictory views cannot all be right. To say otherwise is as illogical as suggesting that red and blue are actually the same colour. It may be politically correct to do so, but it is foolish and an argument that cannot be sustained.

The next step would be to show positively why the Bible is both the word of God and a document that has been handed down to us in a reliable form. We do this by first mentioning that the Bible actually claims to be the word of God. This in itself is not proof, but it is the obvious starting point. Next, we mention that, although the Bible was written by more than forty authors from vastly different backgrounds and cultural perspectives, and although this writing took place over a period of 1200 years, there still remains a single thread throughout, and that thread is God's plan of salvation for humanity.

In addition to this remarkable fact, we need to focus on the prophecies in Scripture, that came true and thus add considerable weight to belief in the inspired nature of the Bible. Indeed, Scripture itself makes it clear that fulfilled prophecy is evidence of the divine origin of the prophecy (Jer. 28: 9; Deut. 18: 21–22). In the Old Testament, there are three kinds of prophecy. First, there are predictions about the coming of the Messiah. Second, there are predictions about kings, nations and cities. Third, there are predictions about the Jews. These predictions are not vague but very specific, even to the point of naming people, places and specific actions. In particular, the prophecies that are linked with the birth, life and death of Jesus Christ are so specific, even though some of them were given nearly a thousand years before the time of Christ, they could not possibly be taken as coincidental.

It is also worth noting that the Bible is largely a book grounded in history. In the Old Testament we read the account of the children of Israel travelling to the Promised Land and then leading a settled existence as a nation. As they do so, they interact with a great many tribes, people groups and empires. There are many events places and people mentioned. The same is true of the New Testament. It tells the story of Jesus and his followers and their exploits against the background of the powerful Roman Empire and many significant world events. The importance of this point is that each historical person, place or event can be cross-referenced with what we know of the history of the ancient world. Evidence of these things can be found through archaeological digs, of which there have been thousands in the Bible lands. The evidence of history or archaeology can either damage the credibility of the Bible or enhance it. It does the latter and not a single event, person or place in the Bible can reliably be discounted. This, too, adds weight to the Bible's claim to be the word of God.

Perhaps the most powerful argument in favour of the Bible being the word of God is the testimony of Jesus on the matter. Jesus unequivocally put his full seal of approval on the Old Testament (Mt. 5: 18) and he continually quoted the Old Testament, applying it to situations that he found himself in. He also stated that his followers would receive divine help, so that they could pass on what they saw and heard for successive generations. The recommendations of Jesus, as well as the comments made by the New Testament writers, clearly demonstrate the divine nature of the New Testament. If Jesus is God, and there is ample evidence to substantiate that claim, and if he declared the Bible to be the word of God, then it must be accepted as such.

There remains one last strand to the argument. How do we know that the biblical text we have in our hands has the same content as the document that was originally penned? After all, none of the original documents (known as autographs) exist today. This is a huge and complex issue, but we have nevertheless good reason for accepting that the documents we have are a reliable record.

When it comes to the Old Testament, we can have a sense of confidence because of the detailed copying methods that the ancient scribes used. The basis for the present text of the Hebrew Bible is the Masoretic text, and this is the prototype against which all other texts are compared. The Masoretes gave painstaking detail to their work of copying the text. As they worked on a scroll, they ensured that each page on the scroll was copied exactly, line for line and word for word. They checked and cross-checked each sheet before it was sewn to the rest of the scroll. When a book was completed, they subjected it to more checks, including how many times each letter of the alphabet occurred in the scroll. Such fine attention to detail results in a very high degree of accuracy in the copying technique. The discovery of the Dead Sea Scrolls has also provided considerable confirmation of the integrity of the copying, as they give comparative texts that are a thousand years older than the Masoretic texts.

We can have confidence in the integrity of the New Testament documents because of the sheer number of manuscripts that we have available to us. There are some 13,000 manuscript copies of whole books or portions that can be compared to each other. This is a far greater number of texts than for any other ancient document. As different manuscripts from distant places are brought together, the level of their similarity is evidence of how far back in time the documents from which these manuscripts were copied are placed. This gives a very clear picture of just how reliable the copies that we possess really are. The embarrassment of wealth in the textual tradition can give us complete confidence in the integrity of the present New Testament text. What we have is faithful to what the authors originally wrote.

Why is Christianity the only way?

I often find that, when I am making headway contending for the truthfulness of Christianity, people respond by accepting that the Christian faith is true, but insist that it is not the only truth. In our postmodern society, not only is everyone's holy scripture valid, but everyone's faith is true for the particular practitioner. We all have our own way of getting to God, but we all get there in the end, and no one can say that their route is the best. It is merely the best for them. This tolerance of diversity is the very essence of postmodernity.

This kind of question is difficult to answer for at least three reasons. First, to contend with a question like this is to attack the very heart of our pluralist society, and therefore Christians who hold to the uniqueness of Christianity are castigated as intolerant bigots. Second, many people who hold to a pluralist worldview are not so much concerned with fact and evidence as with political correctness and the acceptance of others. Third, we are dealing with a profoundly emotional issue, for to say that some faiths are wrong is to say that many sincere and devout Muslims and Hindus are going to a lost eternity. This is, of course, the truth, but it is a doctrine that is unpalatable to most contemporary people.

I would begin dealing with this issue in the same way that I deal with questions about the divine nature of Scripture. When all is said and done, two contradictory ideas cannot both be true. Logically, if they are different, then one must be right and one must be wrong. However unpalatable this may seem in our tolerant society, it simply does not make sense to argue otherwise. I would also point out that most other world religions would also claim that they are true. As Ravi Zacharias notes, 'at the very heart of every religion is an uncompromising commitment to a particular way of defining who God is or is not and accordingly, of defining life's purpose'[4]. The Christian is, therefore, not alone in claiming the uniqueness of his faith.

At this point, I would state that the thing that makes Christianity unique among all the religions of the world is the person of Jesus Christ. Christianity is unique because Jesus is unique. This then focuses the sceptic's mind firmly on the person of Christ, and that is where the focus should remain. The validity of the Christian faith is based on the person of Christ and what he did. If Christ can be seen to be unique, then the uniqueness of Christianity will be self-evident. But in what ways is Christ unique?

First, Jesus is unique because he came into the world without a human father being involved in his conception. He, unlike any other man who has ever lived, was born of a virgin. The issue of the virgin birth is of course doubted by many, but such doubts cannot be sustained. Mary and Joseph could have gained nothing from the claim that the baby Jesus was not actually Joseph's son. The scandal would have been painful for them to bear, and not one they would have willingly endured, were it not for the fact that Jesus was conceived as a result of the activity of the Holy Spirit. Zacharias and Elizabeth would equally have nothing to gain by allowing their son, John the Baptist, to play second fiddle to his younger cousin Jesus, especially in a society where the pecking order within family life was so important. They willingly allowed John to play this role, and even die by the sword, because they knew the miraculous way in which Jesus came into the world. Anyone who attempts to deny the virgin birth must also explain the behaviour of these two couples; but no credible alternative explanation can be found. That makes Jesus unique; for Mohammed, Krishna and Buddha all came into the world as a result of a conventional and ordinary birth.

Second, Jesus is unique for his life was one of utter moral purity. His adversaries continually tried to trip him up and find some way of accusing him, but their efforts were in vain. Jesus himself challenged his opponents to accuse him of sin, but they could not. At his trial, as false witnesses told

---

4 Ravi Zacharias, *Jesus Among Other Gods: The Absolute Claims of the Christian Message*, :Thomas Nelson Inc 2001, p. 7.

all kinds of lies about him, the judge stated that no fault could be found in him. Those who knew him best, his own disciples, confirmed his purity. Peter declared that Jesus committed no sin (1 Pet. 2: 22), while John stated that in him there is no sin (1 Jn. 3: 5).

By their own admission, this could not be said of Mohammed, Buddha or Krishna. Their struggles are recorded within the pages of their own scriptures. In Surahs 47 and 48, Mohammed was told to ask for forgiveness for sin. The Bhagavad Gita describes the dubious exploits of Krishna with the milkmaids. As for the Buddha, the very fact that he had to endure the many rebirths through reincarnation point to many imperfect lives. In each case, their lives were less than completely holy, but Jesus led a life of purity that no one could question.

Third, Jesus is unique because he performed many miracles that can be historically attested. Again, there are those who doubt the miracles of Christ. These doubts can be dealt with by pointing out the reasonableness of the belief in Christ's miracles. The miracles of Jesus were done in a public setting for all to see. This meant that, among those who witnessed these miracles, were opponents of Jesus who clearly would not want to accept their validity, because genuine miracles would in themselves validate Christ's claim to have come from God. Furthermore, Jesus' miracles varied from control over nature to the healing of diseases and even bringing people back from the dead. They were performed over a period of three years and in environments that could not be controlled in the way that magicians control their stage show. Some of Jesus' miracles were openly attested after the event. The healings, for example, were proved to be valid by those who had been healed. It would be hard to convince Lazarus after his resurrection that the miracle that brought him back to life was bogus.

Some sceptics might still argue that those who witnessed Jesus' miracles were primitive people who could easily be hoodwinked by clever conjuring tricks. Even if this were true, it would be hard to see how a carpenter from Nazareth could perform elaborate conjuring tricks on the scale of the feeding of the five thousand, and get away with it. After all, no one actually denied that something marvellous had happened when Jesus performed his miracles. The fact is, however, that those people who saw Jesus performing miracles were not gullible fools. I have already mentioned that many of the people who witnessed the miracles of Jesus were enemies, who would desperately want to prove that all he did was nothing more than a hoax. If their objections could be voiced, then Jesus would no longer be a threat to them. They therefore watched the miracles, not with open minds ready to accept and believe, but with bitter cynicism, desperately hoping to humiliate Jesus and show him to be a fraud. But despite their vehement opposition to Jesus, they simply could not show his miracles to be false. We have no record, either in the Bible or outside of it, which casts any doubt on the reality of the miracles. It is more logical, therefore, to believe that they did indeed happen; and this makes Jesus unique, for the other founders of world religions did not perform miracles which can be historically validated.

Fourth, Jesus is unique because he actually claimed to be God. He did so in several ways. He used the term 'Abba' when addressing God in prayer. This was a term of familiarity rather akin to the modern 'daddy', which no Jew would have dared to use when speaking to God. He claimed that he was the only person who could reveal the Father to men (Matt. 11: 27), and that he himself was the absolute revelation of God (John. 14: 9). He claimed to have power over demonic forces (Luke 11: 20) to be able to perform miracles (Matt. 11: 4,5) and to forgive sin (Luke 5: 20). Jesus also claimed that he controlled the eternal destiny of men (Luke 12: 8,9). All these things could only be done by God, and in claiming them, this is exactly what Jesus was saying about himself. This not only makes Jesus unique; it also forces us to decide what kind of being he was. As C.S. Lewis stated, when you think of the enormity of Jesus' claims, he was either 'a megalomaniac compared with whom Hitler was the most sane and humble of men' or 'a complete lunatic suffering from that form of delusion which undermines the whole mind of man', or he was indeed God'[5].

Fifth, Jesus is unique because he rose from the dead. The resurrection is undoubtedly the greatest miracle associated with the life of Christ. It was one that is remarkable, not least for the fact that Jesus himself predicted the resurrection long before it ever happened (Mt. 16: 21). The central nature of

---

5 C.S. Lewis, *God in the Dock: Essays on Theology and Ethics*, Grand Rapids MI: Eerdmans 1970, p. 81.

the resurrection of Jesus makes it a target for sceptics, some of whom even doubt the veracity of the resurrection accounts. Consequently, it is here that we must begin to argue for the resurrection of Jesus.

Each of the gospel writers states explicitly that an actual bodily resurrection took place and that Jesus came to life and interacted with hundreds of people, before finally ascending to be with his Father in heaven. These accounts are unambiguous in what they claim. Were these men telling the truth or were they not? Our options are limited to three. They were deluded into thinking that Jesus had risen from the dead, or they knew him still to be dead, but deliberately set out to deceive the world, or they were simply giving an accurate record of events of which they were witnesses.

If we take the first of these, that they were deluded, there is a mountain to climb. First, these witnesses were in an excellent position to assess the facts over an extended period of forty days between the resurrection and the ascension. It is highly improbable that they would have remained in a deluded state for all this time. Second, it was not just one person who claimed to have seen Christ raised from the dead but many, because of the multiple resurrection appearances. Furthermore, the physical nature of the encounters with Jesus makes some kind of hallucination highly unlikely. Again, this makes delusion on the part of the eyewitnesses highly improbable. Third, the inability of the enemies of Jesus to produce a body adds weight to the credibility of the eyewitness claims in the gospels. Given that the production of Jesus' body would have brought to an end any Christian claims of resurrection, a conclusion that the Jewish authorities must surely have wanted, their inability to do so reinforces the credibility of the gospel claims. It is evidence by inference that the eyewitnesses were not deluded.

If the gospel writers and their eyewitness counterparts were not deluded, is it possible then that they were simply deceivers? It would mean that they knew perfectly well that Jesus had not been raised from the dead, but deliberately created a myth so that the world would falsely believe in the resurrection. Again, there is a mountain to climb to maintain this proposition. First, if they were simply lying, then they were very foolish, for many of them suffered for a lie. The persecution of Christians in the immediate aftermath of the formation of the Church and up until Constantine was often severe.

Tacitus describes scenes under the Neronian persecution where Christians were clothed in animal skins and thrown to the dogs or smeared in pitch and set alight. Under such punishment it seems highly unlikely that so many Christians, including biblical writers such as James, John and Peter, would be willing to suffer such hardship and death for something they knew to be untrue because they had engineered it.

Second, had the story of the resurrection been made up, it seems strange that it was believed so widely. Indeed, there are no other competing stories within the Church that rival the resurrection story. Had it been a hoax, it would have needed to be brilliantly orchestrated, but there are no signs of this. Indeed, given the persecution of the Church and the fact that so many Christians were fleeing all over the empire, such orchestration would have been impossible.

Third, had the resurrection been a lie, it would speak volumes about the character of those who set out deliberately to deceive. They would have been people of the lowest moral fibre. However, this would fly in the face of everything we know about these people. By and large, they were simple and sincere men who lacked the guile and cunning that a hoax of this magnitude would require.

Fourth, there is the evidence of geography. Early Christian preaching relied heavily on the claims of the resurrection. The sermon preached at Pentecost took place within days of the resurrection and was delivered in the very same city where Jesus was buried. The proximity in time and location would have made a hoax impossible, especially as the Jewish leadership had a vested interest in opposing Christian preaching.

Having concluded that the disciples of Jesus were neither deceived nor deceivers, we now need to look closely at what they actually said with regard to the resurrection. The evidence for the resurrection of Christ is based on four facts, all of which can be historically attested. These are: that he was dead; that he was buried; that the tomb in which he was buried was subsequently found to be empty; and Christ's post-mortem appearances to his followers and to others.

The fact of his death is not difficult to establish. Bearing in mind the flogging he received and the agonies of crucifixion, the suggestion that he merely fainted and later recovered in the cool of the tomb is absurd. In any case, his executioners were professionals who did not make mistakes. When executioners got bored waiting for their victims to die, they broke their legs so that asphyxiation and a swift death would follow. When they came to Jesus, these experienced executioners did not bother to break his legs because they knew him to be dead already. What is more, a spear had been thrust into the side of Jesus, and the gospel records state that blood and water flowed out (John 19: 34). Though the gospel writers could not have been aware of the significance of this, it strongly suggests that Jesus died of heart failure.

The fact of his burial is equally easy to verify. We are told that Jesus was buried in the tomb of Joseph of Arimathea. Joseph was a wealthy and prominent man and a member of the Sanhedrin, the Jewish parliament. There is no way that a prominent figure like Joseph could have his name linked with the scandal of Jesus and his death as a criminal if it were not true. Members of the Sanhedrin were simply too well known to allow false stories to be linked to them without the stories being exposed as false.

Then there are the accounts of the empty tomb. These too can be verified. If a sceptic were to deny the resurrection, he would have to come up with an alternative suggestion as to why the tomb was empty. Given that the Roman guard was stationed around the tomb, the thought of the disciples stealing the body is simply preposterous. The only other people likely to remove the body were the Jewish or Roman authorities, but neither would have anything to gain from doing so. What is more, at Pentecost, the disciples were preaching about the resurrection of Jesus in the very same city where he was crucified and buried. The Jewish leaders would have loved to silence the disciples, as their impact among the Jewish populace was enormous. The Romans, too, would have been uncomfortable about the stir that this kind of preaching was causing. Both parties could have destroyed Christianity forever, even before it began, simply by producing the body of Jesus. They could not do this, because they did not have the body. Given the lack of alternative explanations for the empty tomb, the only acceptable one is that Jesus did indeed rise from the dead.

Finally, there are the post-mortem appearances of Jesus. He appeared to individuals, to small groups, and to 500 people at once. The range of appearances, and the fact that Jesus talked to people and ate with them, rules out the possibility of these appearances being hallucinations. There is also compelling evidence from the testimony of Paul, who opposed the Church but then dramatically changed the whole course of his life, spending his remaining years propagating the gospel. Such a turnaround can only be explained by a resurrection appearance. James, too, was a sceptic even though he was a brother of Jesus. He too changed his mind, became a leader of the church and, according to Josephus, died for his faith in Christ. His dramatic reversal can only be explained if you accept that he saw the risen Christ and was convinced. All this evidence leads to only one conclusion: that Jesus died and was raised from the dead. His return from death undoubtedly makes him unique and this in turn makes Christianity unique.

The role of the Holy Spirit in evangelism

Even when all of this evidence has been presented and all the questions that have been thrown at us have been answered, that in itself is still not enough to bring people to faith in Christ. A good apologist can present a compelling argument in favour of the Christian faith, but he cannot convict a person of sin. This is the work of the Holy Spirit. That being the case, as well as being prepared to answer the many doubts that people throw up, we need to be prayerful, asking God to break through the scepticism of the age and penetrate into people's hearts. Only this will bring about genuine conversions.

Discussion Questions

1. Which of the above questions do you find the most pertinent and why?
2. Which of these questions do you find most difficult to answer and why?
3. Are there any other important questions you have come across, if so what were they and how did you answer them?

CHAPTER 12

Life in a Strange World

Several years ago, we took a sabbatical from ministry and went out as a family for six months to Tanzania. We stayed in the Moshi Christian Children's Centre, which was a real haven for disadvantaged children, many of whom were orphans. It was such a privilege to live in the centre and get to know some of the children as well as the staff. I developed a particularly soft spot for one boy, whose mother had brought him to the centre as a baby and just left him there. No doubt the mother must have had a tough life, to be driven to such an act of desperation. She may well have felt that it was an act of mercy to give her child to someone who could look after him and, if that was the case, it was a noble act borne out of much pain. Nevertheless it was a shocking act, not least because the child was so vulnerable and helpless. It speaks volumes about the terrible inequality in our world when such actions are not out of place, due to the crippling poverty that so many have to endure. It is hard to imagine what it must feel like to be on the receiving end of such a situation: what must the boy have thought, as he was growing up?

I find it interesting that the Bible describes new Christians as babies. They, too, are spiritually vulnerable and need constant care and supervision in the first few weeks and months of their spiritual lives. This will have a number of implications for those who have been witnessing to them and have brought them to a point of commitment. If new Christians are spiritual babies, then the Christians who witnessed to them are the spiritual parents, which is a significant responsibility. What is their role in relation to these new Christians?

Writing to the Thessalonian believers, Paul told this infant church that when he first brought them the gospel, his love for them was such that he and his companions also shared with them their very lives (1 Thess. 2: 8). As their spiritual father, he committed himself to these Christians, rather than remaining aloof and detached, as they came to terms with their new found faith. This is precisely what we must learn to do with new Christians. They need commitment and support from more mature Christians, which will require not only time being spent with them, but constant prayers for them (1 Thess. 1: 2). A quick glance at any of Paul's epistles will reveal the extent of his knowledge of and interest in the affairs of those he influenced for Christ. If this care is not mirrored in our treatment of new Christians, there will be many casualties along the way.

Church is a strange planet to land on

New Christians need more than nurturing and someone to role model the Christian life for them; they also need to be brought gently into the full life of the church. It has become fashionable among some Christians to treat church as if it were an optional extra. This can be seen in the way that they drift from one church to another, according to whatever style of church suits them at a particular time. Church, however, is much more important than this and needs to be taken seriously. Paul reminds us that Christ loved the Church and gave himself for her (Eph. 5: 25). He also tells us that Christians grow and build one another up as they share their lives together as church (Eph. 4: 16). But despite the importance of church, it can still be a daunting place for new Christians.

Every year, we take our Tilsley College students to a large mosque in the heart of Glasgow as part of their missions' course. We want them to gain an understanding of competing worldviews and religions such as Islam, and the mosque trip enables them to meet some Muslim devotees first hand.

I have always found it fascinating to observe the students as they enter this very different environment. They rarely feel comfortable. Most of them have never been to a mosque before, though they have heard a lot about mosques. What they have been told by others is not always accurate. When they get there, they quickly realise that they know no one and feel keenly that they are just visitors. Most of the worshippers have a different style of dress to my students. It is an environment full of strange sounds and smells; a place where everyone else seems to know what they are doing. There are a lot of unspoken rules which strangers will not understand, and events which mystify the uninitiated. All of this makes the students feel profoundly uncomfortable and confused. This is exactly how a new Christian feels when he goes for the first time to a church.

Church really is a strange place to be, if you are unaccustomed to it. Those of us who come from Christian families are not always aware of just how strange a place church is. This is because we grew up with it and feel automatically at home. However, for someone who has not been used to going to church, it is a bit like a foreign land.

To begin with, people in society at large rarely sing together, unless they are at a football match or a rock concert. Church, however, is full of singing, both contemporary songs and ancient hymns. Most people are not used to sitting down for a protracted period of time and listening to a monologue. In most churches, however, sermons are preached weekly and are often fairly lengthy. Most people only dress up if they are going to a party or perhaps to their office job. Many churches, on the other hand, have dress codes which the bulk of the congregation will adhere to (though thankfully this is changing). Most people have only a few close friends, but there are a great many churches, even large ones, where there is a real sense of unity, friendship and camaraderie.

Unwritten laws

This, however, is just the beginning. Every church will have its own unwritten laws and secret language. These laws will be understood by people who have grown up there, but are not known to newcomers. A few years back, I was invited to preach at a church in Denmark. Before I spoke, we celebrated communion, something I do in my home church every week. In this church, they used lots of tiny cups for the communion wine rather than the one shared cup, but as we do the same in my church I was familiar with this set up. The deacon serving the wine approached me first because I was sitting in the front row. I took my little cup and closed my eyes prayerfully. In my church, all the communicants hold their cup until someone gives the signal, and they all drink their wine together. I just assumed this would be the case here also. However, I was to discover that in this church the custom was to drink your wine immediately and give it back to the deacon who is distributing the cups. I heard a forced cough and looked up, only to see the deacon still standing in front of me, waiting for me to get on with it. Embarrassed, I obliged, but no one had told me that this is how it was done in that particular church.

On another occasion I invited an Anglican friend of mine to share communion in a church that I was doing a mission with. He was used to having a minister conduct the service from the front, with all the ritual and trappings that were a part of his tradition. In this Brethren church, lay participation was the norm and the very relaxed nature of the service took him by surprise. What is more the service began with a video clip, the purpose of which was not obvious until it was explained by a fairly scruffy young man, who gave a devotional thought while still sitting in his seat in the middle of the congregation. Then without warning, someone from the back asked for a particular song to be sung. My friend reached for his hymn book and felt a little embarrassed when he discovered that it was not in the book, but the lyrics were being projected on the screen in the front. He had never experienced an open worship format where members of the congregation spontaneously participate in worship, and consequently this experience was bringing him beyond his comfort zone. Suddenly and without warning, everyone stood to their feet to sing. This was one of those unwritten rules that were simply assumed by everyone, but for my friend it increased his discomfort as he rushed to his feet. I smiled at his awkwardness, but also began to realised just how strange the whole experience was proving to be for him.

These are just two of the many examples that illustrate the point. If established Christians find it strange going to churches that they do not usually frequent; if they struggle to understand all the unwritten laws and to interpret the unique language and terminology of a different church, how much more difficult will an unchurched person find it.

There is a sense in which we will never be able to get rid of the customs and idiosyncrasies of church life. Indeed, it would be wrong to do so, because every church must have some structure and a certain individuality. The church will ultimately reflect the people who comprise it, and just as each individual has his or her own idiosyncrasies and taste, so their church consists in some measure of an accumulation of idiosyncrasies. However, there are a couple of things that we need to do when new converts come along to our churches. First, we need to explain what will happen in any given church service, so that there will be the minimum of bemusement or surprise. This is a simple thing, but it can make the difference between a person feeling uncomfortable and out of place, and feeling that it was an interesting as well as a positive experience. In my own church, whenever someone comes for the first time, one of the leaders of the church will welcome them and take a few minutes to explain what will go on in the programme, and why. This simple courtesy has the effect of putting our visitors at ease.

A second thing we must do is to ensure that what we do in church is thoroughly biblical. Of course there will be many traditions in every church that never get a mention in the Bible. Many churches, for example, delegate someone to stand at the front door to welcome everyone as they come in. You never read about this practice in the Bible, though I think it is a good one. Almost all churches use hymn books or more commonly data projection, which were never available in New Testament times. These traditions are actually helpful and logical. However, some churches insist on traditions that are neither logical nor helpful. These have no biblical justification. Sooner or later, new converts will ask the question why? If there is no biblical justification for these things, then why do we do them? Worse still these traditions become so much part of the church life, changing them seems tantamount to heresy. Too many of these meaningless traditions will lead to frustration and confusion, and will be a disincentive to really engage with church.

One example that comes to mind is the times of church services. Some years ago, I was in a church that conducted a family service every Sunday at 11:30 am. This proved to be a bad time, because most families wanted to make the most of the day, so a one-hour service that did not finish until after midday was not a big attraction. It was unlikely, therefore, that any non-Christians would ever come to this service. It was suggested that the service could be made earlier, either 9:30 or 10:00 am. This inevitably meant that the communion service had to be shifted to an evening slot, or included in the family service or a mixture of both. Unfortunately, there was great resistance to this move, despite the fact that it was so logical. The reason for the opposition was not because of biblical principles—frankly there were none—it was just that things had always been done this way, and the tradition took precedence over common sense and Scripture. For those who had always grown up in the church this did not seem ridiculous, but for those church members who were new to the place the whole issue was utterly absurd. No wonder! Such unbiblical traditions make no sense at all and are damaging if they are counterproductive. It was inevitable that this conflict would discourage many of the new Christians and make them feel that the Bible was not as valued as it should be. This unfortunate situation needs to be avoided at all cost, as it will inevitably lead to disillusionment and will hamper growth both in the lives of individuals and in the church as a whole.

Another aspect of church life that we need to explain to new Christians is what the church actually does. Not only do new Christians struggle to understand all the traditions of church life, they also take a while to fully comprehend what church is all about. They are aware that there is an expectation on them to attend weekly, and they recognise the commitment that this implies, but the big question is why should they be there? The importance of what the church does needs to be spelt out, and new converts need help to appreciate the significance of the church's role.

Although the church does many things, there are four aspects of church life that need particularly to be identified and explained to those being nurtured. These are teaching, fellowship, worship and witness; and they can be seen in the life of the early church (Acts 2: 42–47).

Teaching

The need for teaching within the church is self-evident. Christianity is an intelligent faith that is based on truths, communicated to us through the Bible. However unfashionable sermons may be, there is no getting away from the fact that God's word does need to be taught if the church is to learn how to live and serve God. For new Christians, however, the average sermon will often be a little above their heads. This cannot be avoided because the rest of the church needs to be spiritually fed as well. What is more, it is important to create a whole culture in church of engaging seriously with Scripture and working hard to understand and apply it. However, if some of the new Christians we deal with are not accustomed to going to church before their conversion, the very act of sitting and listening to a half-hour sermon may in itself be daunting for them. They will need to be primed and prepared for this.

There are a few steps that we can teach them, in order to help them get the most out of the sermon. For example, they can pray before the service and ask God to help them understand what is being said. They can also read the Bible passage beforehand, and then note how the preacher unpacks it. Keeping the Bible open during the sermon, so as to follow the logic of the passage, is also helpful. If they are encouraged to take notes during the sermon, they can review them afterwards. They can also be encouraged to note down every question that arises in their minds as the preacher is speaking. These can be put to the preacher at the end of the service, and this will prove helpful to preacher and listener alike. It can also be helpful to have a Q&A session as part of the sermon; this would benefit established Christians as much as new ones. It is also very useful if there is the opportunity after the sermon for church members to discuss the sermon informally. In our church, we link our house group studies with the Sunday sermon, so that this can be done in a structured and systematic way. The one thing we must not do is give the impression that preaching is too much for a new Christian to cope with. It is important to develop good habits quickly, and engaging with the Bible through the church's teaching programme is one such good habit. In my experience, new Christians who are encouraged to study the Bible grow and become strong.

Even when you encourage new Christians in this way, they will still need teaching appropriate to their level. My personal feeling is that a one-to-one discipleship course is the ideal, though if there are several new Christians a small group discipleship course would also be good. There are three reasons why this is important. First, it demonstrates to the new Christians that they are valued and worth investing time solely in them. Second, their personal spiritual needs are catered for and their questions are dealt with. Third, the person doing the discipleship course with them will be a spiritual mentor and will be ideally placed to role-model a Christian lifestyle.

The key factor in such a discipleship course will be to teach material that is appropriate to the needs of the new Christian. For example, it will be entirely inappropriate to teach new converts about prophecy, or frameworks for interpreting Scripture such as dispensationalism, or even about the latest evangelical fads. They are simply not at that stage in their Christian lives. On the other hand, it will be appropriate to teach them about the Christian lifestyle, prayer, the assurance of salvation and the work of the Holy Spirit, personal commitment, witnessing and conquering bad habits. These basics are what they need to grasp quickly, so that they can begin to grow and be protected. One of my friends pointed out to me that in India, where he is a missionary, they begin by teaching new converts about the life and teachings of Jesus. Passages like the Sermon on the Mount have a great deal to say about the basic issues of Christian living. Such a teaching programme also fits into the command that Jesus himself gave in his Great Commission, that we should teach everything that he taught (Matt. 28: 20). This seems eminently sensible.

As well as teaching new Christians, we need to encourage them to read the Bible for themselves and develop practical habits of personal prayer. There are many Bible reading plans and devotional notes that will prove to be useful. I also think it is valuable to encourage new Christians to get into the habit of reading through the whole Bible on a regular cycle. With 1189 chapters, the Bible will seem an impossibly daunting book, but there are some Bible reading plans that take the reader through the Bible by picking out just a few key chapters here and there. This will enable the same objective to be reached within a less daunting framework. From a practical point of view, I would also encourage them to use a very accessible Bible version such as the New Living Version.

Worship

Another important aspect of church life is that of worship. Here, too, a different world opens up to new Christians. For those of us who have grown up in churches or who have been Christians for a long time, collective worship can be a wonderful experience. Our knowledge of God fills us with a sense of awe that compels us to worship. We understand the worship traditions of our own church and can easily fit into the mindset of structured worship. We may also have learned to appreciate the particular form of worship in our own local church. For a new Christian, however, especially one with no experience of church life, public worship can be a daunting and even confusing experience.

New Christians certainly understand that Christ died for them and has saved them, but they will probably not appreciate the sheer greatness of God. The attributes of omnipresence, omniscience and omnipotence will be a mystery to them. Their knowledge and appreciation of these things will require time to grow. When it does, their sense of wonder and desire for worship will also grow, but this takes time. They will also be unfamiliar with the worship experience and format of their new church.

I grew up within a Christian Brethren tradition, where members of the congregation participate in public worship. In a typical worship service, someone opens the service by reading a passage of Scripture that sets the theme for the service. Those participants who are familiar with the format then make their contribution to the worship service, and generally keep to the theme set by the person who opened the service. Of course, no official rule stated that participants follow this theme, but it is a tradition that developed over many years of church practice. On one occasion, a Christian friend who was not familiar with this tradition came to our church and participated in the service by asking for a hymn to be sung and then praying. What he said in his prayer was very real and helpful, as was the hymn which he requested, but it did not fit in with the overall theme of the service. This was not his fault, for he did not understand the unwritten rules of that type of worship. Some of the older members of the congregation, though very appreciative of his contribution, nevertheless put the whole experience down to his spiritual immaturity. Not so! He was just not used to the particular ethos, style and customary content of worship in that particular congregation. A new Christian who has never been to church before will be in exactly the same position.

When it comes to acclimatising new Christians to the concept of worship, there are a number of things we need to stress. First, it is important that they know that a life committed to God is an act of worship in itself. Indeed what we do during a worship service is irrelevant—and indeed unacceptable to God—if the life we live outside of church is a denial of Christ. Worship is therefore something we do every day.

Second, our worship needs to be sincere. However much or little we understand about God and his will, he knows us intimately and can read our very thoughts. Those of us who have been Christians for years know how easy it is to become complacent in our worship. If we are not careful, it is all too easy to slip into a habit of singing songs that we do not think about, or to say 'Amen' at the end of a prayer that we have not even listened to. It is engaging our minds and hearts, and expressing our profound gratitude to God, that is at the very heart of worship. This needs to be done with utter sincerity. New Christians need to know that even the most bumbling expressions of thanks, offered sincerely from a pure heart, are more important than the most polished phrases or theologically-correct expressions.

Third, we need to communicate to new Christians that worship is an intelligent exercise. Worship should never be cold and purely rational, but if we are to express our appreciation of the greatness of God, we need to know who he really is. In that sense, worship is closely related to theology. Without an understanding of God, our worship can become a repetitive series of bland platitudes that say nothing about the God we claim to adore. I have met several couples that claim that when they met it was love at first sight. I don't doubt they found each other attractive at first sight, but love is something that grows as you get to know a person. It is when we really get to know God and grasp something of the wonder of who he is that our worship becomes enlivened and intelligent. When we run discipleship classes for new Christians, we must take this into consideration.

Fourth, we need to communicate that true worship involves emotion. God has given us feelings, and these are to be used within the context of worship. These feelings will enable us to get excited about God and empress our appreciation of him enthusiastically. Though we need to teach new Christians to express their emotions appropriately, they also need to give vent to their emotions and to recognise that they are a natural vehicle for expressing how we feel about God. If there is no sense of awe as we approach our majestic God, and no sense of wonderment and excitement when we think of all that he has done for us, then there is something profoundly wrong with our spiritual walk.

Prayer

Another area where orientation will be necessary is that of prayer. Again, for people who have been Christians for a long time, prayer is something that comes naturally and easily. But, for a new Christian, prayer can be an extremely difficult thing. However, as prayer is at the very heart of the Christian life, this is an area to which much attention must be focused.

Emphasising the beauty of prayer is where this orientation must begin. By prayer we enter the immediate presence of God without the need of any intermediaries. The moment we pray God hears every word and begins responding to our plans. This fellowship with our Father is essential for spiritual health and it is for this reason that the Bible encourages us to pray continually (1 Thess. 5: 17). This knowledge, in itself, does not make prayer any easier, but an awareness of the necessity of prayer will encourage new Christians to work hard at it.

I have often found that it is necessary to pray with new Christians, so they can hear for themselves how natural it is. It is interesting that Jesus' disciples asked him to teach them to pray (Luke 11: 1). They were religious Jews, who would have heard prayer in their local synagogue all their lives. However, when they heard Jesus pray, they realised that prayer is much more than just a repetition of some well-worn phrases. It was all about a living relationship with God in which we communicate with each other. In much the same way, we need to coach new Christians in prayer and model it to them. As we do so, it is helpful to encourage them to relax and be themselves in prayer. They do not need to use any formal words or phrases, but just talk to God in language they normally use in conversation. As the habit grows, words will come more readily.

I would like to suggest some guidelines, which could give new Christians some structure to their prayer lives:

- Discipline yourself to spend at least 15 minutes each day reading your Bible and praying. Ensure that this is a priority!
- Find somewhere quiet where you can pray without interruptions or distractions.
- Begin your prayer time by thanking God for all he has been doing in your life and worship him for who he is.
- pray out loud if that is helpful to you. This will help you concentrate and think about what you are saying.
- Keep a prayer diary, so that you can list the kind of things you should be praying about and then cross off the list any prayers that have been answered. This will help you pray consistently and encourage you as you see prayers answered.

These points are very simple and routine, but they are helpful ways of encouraging new Christians to pray during the early months of their Christian life.

Witness

A fourth area where new Christians need help is when it comes to witnessing to others. As they begin in their newfound faith they will discover that people will relate to them in different ways. Some of their friends will snigger and think the whole thing is a little silly. Others will oppose and openly criticise them. Still others will be ambivalent and in some cases, be very pleased for them. It will be important to prepare them for every possible reaction and to encourage them to talk openly to their friends about the decision they have made. Once the news of their new-found faith is out in the open, they will be vulnerable to the opinions of their friends, but they will have made their first stand as Christians.

New Christians need to do more than just be open about their faith. They need to learn to share it with others. This can be very daunting indeed, and they will need your support as they take their first few steps as witnesses for Jesus Christ. There are, of course, many examples of people who become

Christians and are so fired up and enthusiastic about their faith that they need no encouragement to witness. They do so boldly and seem to want to tell the whole world that they have trusted in Jesus. When this is the case it is wonderful, but even then they need some input, so that when they witness they will do so tactfully and with grace and wisdom.

I remember some years ago, while working in the Republic of Ireland, coming across a young Christian from a small country town near where I was staying. He had been a Christian for only a couple of years, and, though an enthusiastic evangelist, he was already running into serious trouble. The town in which he grew up was almost entirely Roman Catholic, and a very conservative brand of Catholicism was practised. Once this young man became a Christian, he grew very angry that in all his years of faithfully attending the Roman Catholic Church he had never heard a clear presentation of the gospel. He was determined to share the good news with every person in the town so that they too could find true faith. His motives were pure and his enthusiasm commendable. His methodology, however, left much to be desired. He wrote to publishers in the USA looking for tracts that would be 'anti-Catholic'. When he found one, he bought 10,000 copies and distributed them to every house in the district. The particular tract he used was very offensive, and the whole population was outraged to the point where he had become an outcast. This problem could have been avoided had he been given some guidance as a young Christian about how to witness.

One of the important things to bear in mind when working with young Christians is that they have all the contacts. Inevitably, the longer a person goes to church and gets involved in the life of the church, the more Christians he will befriend. Conversely, this will almost always mean that he will have fewer close friends who are non-Christians. As I mentioned earlier in this book, when I deliver my evangelism lectures at Tilsley College, I ask my students to make a list of their ten closest friends. Then I ask them to put a mark next to the ones who are Christians. In most cases the vast majority of their close friends will be Christians. In some cases it is also possible to see a fairly strong link between the length of time a person has been involved in church life and the number of close friends he has who are non-Christians.

When a person first becomes a Christian, in all probability most of his closest friends will not be Christians. This can be a pressure and because of that the church needs to learn to support him, especially in the very early days and weeks of his faith. However, it is also a great opportunity to reach his peer group with the gospel. This will involve his living a consistent Christian life in front of them and tactfully sharing what Christ means to him, especially when questions are raised. In order for both of these things to be achieved, the church will actively need to provide advice and support.

Discussion Questions

1. What aspects of the life of your church would someone who is un-churched find the most difficult?
2. Of the four functions of church mentioned above, evaluate how well your church does at each and what could be done to improve on them?
3. What practical steps can you take to ensure you are a welcoming church?

CHAPTER 13

Heavy Loads and Ugly Ducklings

I have long decided that travel is much less fun than people imagine. While it is true that modern technology has made travel both cheaper and more accessible, it has not necessarily made it much more pleasant. Flying is my particular pet hate, mostly because I do so much of it. Airports, especially regional ones, are boring, soul destroying, expensive and with very few comfortable chairs. Budget airlines are an equal trial, with seats that do not recline and levels of legroom that make it difficult for anyone over five foot six.

Perhaps the thing that annoys me most about travel is the baggage that I need to take with me, which can often be cumbersome. No matter how well you pack your case, the many security checks you have to go through in the post 9/11 world ensure that it will be a dishevelled mess by the time you reach your destination. More worrying still is the fact that larger cases are taken off you and become the responsibility of the airline. How they handle this baggage becomes a concern. I have arrived in Copenhagen airport, only to discover that my suitcase was in Singapore, and so had to spend four days in the same clothes. I also arrived back from a flight from DR Congo to discover that my soft-skinned case had been torn open and some of the contents missing. I even remember taking an internal flight from Addis Ababa to the northern Ethiopian town of Kombolcha, where the airport is just a field full of cattle, and witnessing the aircrew throwing the bags out of an open door and landing on the ground with a bump. The handling of baggage certainly varies, and sometimes can cause a great deal of damage.

When it comes to church life there are plenty of people who carry baggage around with them. Many people have skeletons in the cupboard and issues that spill over from their past life, which they struggle to deal with. The church cannot ignore this baggage. It can be very weighty, and some churches have been guilty of treating it with the same rough contempt that airport handlers treat their baggage. Whether we like it or not, however, the baggage is there, it will not go away and needs to be dealt with. If we, as churches, are serious about evangelism at all, then we need to learn to be good baggage handlers.

Moral baggage

There are two main types of baggage that need to be dealt with, and both present us with a huge challenge. First, there is moral baggage and, second, there is emotional baggage. Moral baggage is those issues which affect a person's life because of sin. Much of this baggage, of course, would not be perceived by our relativistic society as a problem. We live in a society where the use of recreational drugs, drunkenness, homosexuality, pre-marital sex, cross-dressing and foul language are considered to be the norm rather than things that are morally questionable. Indeed, in our postmodern world the word morality is going out of fashion. People do not do wrong things; they do not sin; they merely make lifestyle choices. What one person decides is right, another might object to; but this is a personal choice as opposed to a moral issue.

We, as Christians, have a very different way of looking at morality, as indeed do other world faiths. We believe in an objective set of values, based on the character of God and revealed to us in Scripture. The problem is that, as unchurched people become Christians, they may be completely unaware of these values and may already be tangled up in a lifestyle that is a far cry from a biblical one. Some of these lifestyle issues may be ingrained and highly complex. I recently took a phone call from a friend whose church was visited by a woman called Diana, who claimed to have become a Christian and was looking for fellowship with other Christians. My friend, who was an elder, made her feel welcome and explained to her that the service she had turned up to was a communion service and that, if she genuinely had faith in Jesus, she was welcome to participate. As the service wore on he suddenly realised that she had some facial stubble. He discovered after the service that Diana was born David, has spent several years as a cross-dresser before having gender relocation surgery, and now was living as a woman. He had no doubt that Diana was definitely a Christian, he just wasn't sure what to do next in terms of supporting her spiritually.

The question could well be asked of Diana, and indeed any other new convert who was struggling with lifestyle issues: did they really repent and become Christians, and if so why is there still an issue about their lifestyle? However, we need to be careful not to be too simplistic about the way we handle complex issues. First, the person you are dealing with may not even be aware that some of their actions were sinful, even though they are a Christian. We simply cannot assume that all new Christians have a finely tuned Judeo-Christian ethic. One friend of mine, who became a Christian, was co-habiting with his girlfriend in a long term monogamous relationship. His repentance at his conversion was genuine, and he earnestly tried to stop doing things he knew to be sin. However, he genuinely did not realise that co-habitation could be an issue. In his culture, as in much of the West, marriage was the exception rather than the norm. His problem was not that he was rebelling deliberately against the will of God, quite the reverse! He just had no idea that what he was doing was sin.

This kind of problem will, I believe, become ever more common in the future, for a couple of reasons. First, with morality being increasingly relativized in society, we will get more and more people coming to faith in Christ from a background where there is no recognition of right and wrong. These people will have repented because they will have recognised that they have sinned in some way. However, their concept of sin will be vague, and there will be many things, like cohabitation and homosexuality, that they will not regard as sin, because their culture does not.

Second, in our experience-orientated culture, there will be more and more people who want to become Christians because they want the experience of being a Christian, rather than because they want to repent and rid themselves of the guilt of sin. In other words, they are positively attracted to a relationship with a loving God rather than coming to that God in repentance because of fear of judgment. This will particularly be the case when they see how well their Christian friends have coped with crisis and heartbreak in their lives. They will find Christianity attractive because they find their Christian friends to be attractive people. This does not mean that repentance has never featured in their conversion, but that it has played a relatively minor part. People who become Christians in these circumstances will inevitably go through some kind of culture shock, as they discover that they need to live a lifestyle that is holy.

The big question is how we deal with people who become Christians but have significant moral baggage. People are, of course, complex beings, and therefore their lives will inevitably be complex. Anyone who suggests that these problems are easy to deal with, or that there are simple answers to the problem, has obviously never really been involved in pastoral work. Let me give a few examples to illustrate the kind of complexities involved.

After attending a series of family services, a family man called Gerald became a Christian. The church was delighted and immediately began a discipleship class, with a view to baptising this new convert and bringing him into church membership. The family setting seemed ideal, as Gerald gave the appearance of a happily married man with four lovely children. Gerald's wife showed little interest in becoming a Christian, but she was impressed with the changes that had taken place in her husband's life and thought that his going to church was a good thing. During one of the discipleship classes Gerald mentioned that he and his 'wife' had never actually been married. They had just cohabited for sixteen years and had never seen the need for marriage. It was put to Gerald that he really should be married before he could come into membership and, reluctantly, he agreed to talk to his partner about it. She reacted very badly, insisting that a legal document would not make their relationship any better, and stating that she felt insulted that he should try and revoke a decision they had made years ago, just because the church was interfering. Her attitude to the church began to change, as she regarded it with a new suspicion.

In another case a self-employed businessman called Michael became a Christian through the witness of a Christian who was involved in the same industry. Again, the setting seemed so ideal. This new Christian had a good job and a family and seemed to be a pillar of the community. It turned out, however, that Michael had been fiddling the books for many years, so as to avoid paying taxes. This kind of behaviour was so common and acceptable that he had never thought of it as being morally dubious. Indeed he argued that the government could not be trusted to deal with his taxes properly, so his manipulation of figures in his tax return was a way of protecting himself and his family. His whole lifestyle, and the many bills which his lifestyle caused, meant that tax evasion was virtually a necessity. Without it, he would have to make substantial reductions in his spending which in turn would cause great difficulties in his already struggling marriage.

A third case involved a woman in her mid-thirties who made a commitment to Christ. Jean had twice been married and divorced. One probable reason for the short-lived relationships was the residual effect of a difficult family background. Her father was physically and verbally abusive, and that had left her badly scarred and emotionally damaged to the point where she struggled to trust men or have a stable relationship with them. Financially she was struggling, and this was made worse by the fact that she had two growing boys to look after. Jean had an affair with a married man who was estranged from his wife. Her desperation for security and love drove her to continue this relationship, even though she was not convinced that she loved the man. He was in the process of getting a divorce and, at the time of her conversion, they were making the final plans for their marriage.

The last example involves John, who is a single man in his early twenties. He is homosexual and has had a number of relationships in the past, though at the time of his conversion he was not involved with anyone. Because of the homophobic attitudes that John felt were rife in his area, he began to gravitate in his social life towards other homosexuals. He felt safer and more accepted in bars and clubs where he would meet people with his own orientation. He obtained a mortgage that put him under considerable financial pressure, and therefore wanted to find a lodger who would help to share the bills. He did not mind whether his lodger was male or female, though, given his social life, the possibility of finding a lodger who was male and homosexual was really quite high. By the time John became a Christian, he had found a lodger, another homosexual man, though at that time they were not involved in a relationship with each other, it was merely an accommodation agreement. John began attending church but with a considerable degree of trepidation, as he had always believed that the church was a thoroughly homophobic institution.

How should churches deal with issues like these? How soon in our discipleship classes should we begin to deal with the moral baggage in people's lives? Should we require these new Christians to get their lives sorted out before they can become church members, and should they be able to participate in church services or take communion until this has happened?

Finding answers to these questions is notoriously difficult. By their very nature they are complex, and the implications of any decision will necessarily be profound. There is no such thing as a simple solution when dealing with people's lives. Each church will also have particular practices which have a bearing. For example, in my church, it is possible to take the sacraments, that is be baptised and take communion, without actually becoming a member. In other churches, being baptised is tantamount to becoming a member and Christians cannot take part in communion without first being members of the church. Some churches even find themselves in the situation where a significant number of their members are not Christians anyway. Nevertheless, given that all our churches will be different and have their own distinctives, there are some principles which we can identify that will help us is answering the basic question: what do we do with new Christians who carry a great deal of moral baggage with them?

Don't run

The first thing we must do is ensure that we don't run away from any issue. Unfortunately, many churches do just this. They do not want the hassle of trying to find answers to intractable problems, and do not have the courage to grasp the nettle in dealing with people's lives. As a result, they tend to try to get rid of the problem altogether. This is done in a variety of ways, ranging from telling the person directly that they are not welcome, to implying this by a generally unwelcoming attitude.

This, of course, is the easiest way to proceed. When churches do this, they no longer have to face the problems that are caused by evangelism. It is a neat and tidy way of running a church, with no awkward customers to handle. But there are two fundamental problems with this approach. First, it is entirely unchristian for a church to behave in this way. Jesus had no hesitation helping people in need, even to the point where he was labelled a friend of sinners. To reject people because they present problems is to turn our backs on Christ-like compassion. Second, it is a very short-sighted policy. Given the moral decline in our society, it is unlikely that our evangelistic efforts will produce many converts with little or no moral baggage. Most people live lives that are a far cry from biblical standards, because they live in a society that has altogether ignored what the Bible has to say. If churches insist on making it difficult for people like this to become part of the church, then the possibility of growth will greatly diminish. Consequently, churches that are intolerant are churches that, in general, are dying out. The sterile atmosphere that these churches create kills off all life.

Biblical standards

A second thing we must do in our churches is to maintain biblical standards. Although intolerance is not the answer, neither is compromise. The church in every age has to be aware of the danger of being assimilated into the world. Never is this danger more acute than when significant numbers of new converts bring with them their moral baggage. Indeed, one of the unfortunate consequences of many revivals is that the church has become increasingly immoral in their immediate aftermath.

A balance needs to be maintained. The church needs to lovingly embrace new converts, with all their baggage, while at the same time communicating the clear message that we, as Christians, need to live God-honouring lives. If the standards which the church expects of its members begin to slip, that church will inevitably lose its cutting edge and moral authority. This in turn will also lead to a slow death. A church with no standards will not be able to distinguish itself from the world around it. It will therefore not be in a position to call people out of the world. Having no standards, therefore, is just as unbiblical and short-sighted as intolerance towards new Christians with baggage.

Of course bringing these two things together presents practical problems. It means that church leaders could be preaching lofty moral values from the pulpit, while at the same time showing empathy and understanding to people whose lives are in a moral mess. This could appear to be a contradiction and hypocrisy. However, it is not; though the tension between these two positions is not an easy one to deal with. Church leaders will need to ask for and obtain the trust of church members as they deal with these issues. Great wisdom and much prayer is a must. The best model of this balance can be seen in the example of Jesus. During Christ's ministry, he not only rubbed shoulders with people whose lives were in an intractable moral mess, he also dealt with their problems as they made their first few steps towards faith. As recorded in John 8, a woman was brought before Jesus having committed the act of adultery. The Pharisees who brought her asked Jesus for his opinion on whether or not she should be stoned to death for her crime, as demanded by the law of Moses.

Jesus brilliantly parried their attempt to trap him, and then focused his attention on the woman herself. His words to her were beautiful and strong. He first told her that he did not condemn her, even though he knew of her guilt. This brings to mind Jesus' statement that he came not to condemn but to save, (John 3:17; 12:47). Having said that, Jesus went on to insist that this woman's proper response to mercy should be to stop sinning. Here we have a picture of Christ forgiving and refusing to condemn, but balancing this with the insistence that a holy life is a must and that real progress is expected. This balance is not easy to maintain, but the church needs to learn to imitate Christ.

Remember they are babies

A third thing that we need to bear in mind is that new Christians are spiritual babies (1 Pet. 2: 2). It would be entirely unreasonable to expect a baby to drive a car, hold down a secure job or work out their income tax. This kind of activity can only be done with a measure of maturity. Babies and children also have to be taught what is right and wrong, as their sense of values is in need of fine-tuning. Parents therefore do not let their children make big decisions for themselves until they are capable of doing so.

In much the same way, the Bible pictures new Christians as spiritual babies. They are not in a position to make mature and informed decisions about their lifestyles. They obviously want to follow Christ, and have repented, but that does not mean that they understand what is appropriate or inappropriate behaviour for a Christian. They will also be inclined to make mistakes and fall, just as normal babies do. In addition, adults who become Christians do not begin their Christian lives within a vacuum. Rather, their starting point is at a time when bad habits have already been formed and attitudes about what is right and wrong are calcified. In that sense there us a great deal to unlearn before they can really begin to learn about the Christian life.

We should not be surprised, then, if new Christians struggle to lead holy lives and find it very difficult to break the sinful habit patterns of the past. The church should not condemn them, but should care for them as parents, and re-educate them so that they can begin to live holy lives. This may take some time! Spiritual maturity and the discernment that it brings do not come about overnight. I have worked with Christians who have been struggling with big moral issues in their lives for years after their conversion. While not compromising on the standards that it expects, the church needs to demonstrate patience, and not develop the attitude that new Christians should be pounced upon as soon as they make a mistake. If a new convert does get drunk, stumbles sexually or behaves unwisely, it does not invalidate his claim to be a follower of Christ. Rather, it means that, as a spiritual baby, he is struggling to come to terms with his newfound faith. These issues need to be handled lovingly and sensitively.

The wider picture

Fourth, each person within the church is an individual, and each case needs to be taken on its own merits. As a church we need to be aware, when we are dealing with young Christians and their problems, which wider issues may be involved, and other people need to be taken into consideration. Take the case of Gerald as an example. Although he was living with a woman to whom he was not married, and had children by her, his wife was not a Christian and therefore could not be expected to have a biblical view of marriage. Certainly the church leaders would be wise to explain to Gerald's wife why the church values marriage so much. However, they would have no authority to demand that she agree to marriage, neither should Gerald be coerced into putting her under any pressure, as this could jeopardise their relationship. In such a situation there is no right answer, but there are wrong ones. In my judgment, it would be wrong to deny Gerald membership of the church, even though his relationship is clearly wrong. He was in a situation that had wider ramifications and these needed to be taken into consideration. In many situations, you will not be able to find a win-win solution because it doesn't exist, but you can avoid causing significant damage and this should be your goal.

Acute and chronic problems

A final thing that we need to consider is whether or not this issue is something that is an on-going habit pattern, or it is just a mistake that the new Christian has made. In one sense, it should make no difference, because sin is sin. On the other hand, a person's intention needs to be taken into account.

Take the issue of drunkenness for example. In our society, the excessive consumption of alcohol is hardly unknown. Indeed, for many, the weekend is reserved for binge drinking and hangovers. There is a difference between someone who regularly gets drunk, and has the intention of doing so, and someone who has an occasional drink and perhaps consumes a little too much. In both cases, there is a degree of intoxication, but one is certainly more serious than the other and, pastorally, must be treated as such. I know a number of young Christians who come from homes where alcohol is available in abundance and where family members are often drunk. If a young Christian in such circumstances were to get drunk regularly it would be a cause of great concern, and the church would certainly have to exercise discipline. However, if that same person occasionally made a mistake and took too much, given the whole culture of drinking from which they came, I think a little understanding would be more appropriate than the heavy hand of discipline. I am not saying that getting drunk is acceptable for a Christian, nor am I saying that this should not receive pastoral attention. But I am differentiating between a chronic problem and one which is no more than a regrettable incident.

These guidelines do not in themselves answer the question of how we deal with new Christians who bring with them a great deal of moral baggage. These issues are still very difficult to deal with, and often our response should be one of damage limitation, as no perfect solution exists. However, if applied, these guidelines will help a church to move forward, taking each case on its own merits, and cutting a path along which the church and the new Christian can proceed to their mutual benefit.

One crucial element that must not be lost sight of is the necessity of these new Christians growing in their faith. These issues are best worked out if the new Christian begins to develop spiritual maturity. The key to seeing this growth, and a biblical lifestyle emerging as a result, is for more mature Christians to role model the Christian life and mentor their young brothers and sisters in Christ. There is no substitute for a Christian friend who is close enough to the person to see what is needed, and encouraging enough to enable the person to take steps towards spiritual maturity.

Emotional baggage

Another type of baggage is the emotional sort. This, too, is on the increase. I have long been of the opinion that most people, emotionally speaking, are held together by scar tissue. Life takes its toll on people in the modern world. Work pressures, family crises, marital breakdown, abuse and bereavement have left many people wounded and hurting. A significant proportion of people who become Christians will carry some of these hurts with them into their new-found faith. Indeed, throughout history the church has often been perceived by society as a caring place, a sanctuary where life's victims can find comfort and acceptance. This is good, because it demonstrates that the church has fulfilled its role of caring for those for whom no one else cares. But the result of this has been that the church has often attracted people who are damaged emotionally. If we are serious about evangelism we should not be surprised if we end up with at least some church members who are troubled, suffer from stress and marital problems and have bouts of depression requiring counselling and anti-depressants.

The pastoral burden that many churches have to carry is both enormous and growing—indeed, it is a virtually bottomless pit. In our postmodern age people are very absorbed with their own needs and have a great desire to share these needs with others. Indeed a recent edition of Time magazine warned about the growing tide of narcissism that comes as part and parcel of the millennial generation (*Time*, May 20, 2013, pp. 28-35). This desire for 'opening up' and sharing feelings is so strong that the talk shows have turned people's problems into a voyeuristic art form. Discussing your problems with individuals or an audience is the therapy of this new millennium. My eldest daughter tells me that one of the most popular programmes among her peers is the Jeremy Kyle show.

Anyone who is involved in church leadership will confirm that increasing numbers of people in our churches want to bring their burdens to the leadership of the church, in the hope of finding help. No longer do people put up with it and keep a stiff upper lip. Rarely do we meet people who want to suffer in silence. The openness of our culture has brought everyone's skeletons out of the cupboard and into public gaze.

In much the same way as some churches struggle to deal with all the moral baggage that comes their way, they also stagger under the weight of all the emotional baggage. This baggage is often roughly treated by Christian leaders, intolerant of the needs of those to whom they minister. I have heard horror stories of wounded people who have sought help from the leaders of their church only to be told to 'get a grip' of themselves and stop attention-seeking. In some cases, this response comes from leaders who feel overwhelmed by the great need and their increasing pastoral responsibilities. Sadly, in other cases it is simply because leaders can sometimes be impatient and lacking in genuine compassion.

How do we begin to deal with the enormous pastoral issues that arise? This is a huge issue, because if we do not lovingly care for the new converts that come to our churches for sanctuary, they will leave concluding that the church is not a place for them after all. Once bitten, they will be unlikely ever to return to church, as they have received the message that church only accepts people who come with no baggage or problems. So how do we deal with these emotional problems?

Don't duck any problems

The first thing we must do, as we care for emotionally damaged people, is ensure that we ignore no one. In much the same way as we avoid people who carry moral baggage with them, it is easy to avoid people with emotional problems. This should never be the case. In some cases, people present problems that to the casual observer seem trite and insignificant. To the person to whom it is a problem, however, it may well be a big issue. It should therefore not be treated as something trivial. Other problems are much more serious and demand a great deal of thought and attention. This must be given, recognising that everyone is precious in God's sight and is loved by him. In short no one should be ignored.

Be prepared for the long haul

A second thing that needs to be borne in mind is that people are not machines that can be fixed quickly. My car, though old, is able to function well with the occasional oil change and a bit of servicing. If anything goes wrong, my friends at the local garage can have it fixed in a matter of hours. Not so with people. We are highly complex beings and our emotional make-up is full of complexity. Some people have the capacity to bounce back after problems and keep going, others simply cannot. Some of the people who come to our churches will be carrying emotional scars that run deep and have been causing pain for years. It is entirely unrealistic to imagine that these issues will disappear after a few weeks of loving church fellowship. Certainly, the warmth of church life is of great help to people who are struggling, but the scars can take years to heal. The work of pastoral care is very long-term indeed, and will require considerable patience and perseverance.

Treat every person with sensitivity

It goes without saying that the wounded people who come to us need to be treated with sensitivity. They are already suffering, and do not need curt remarks or an attitude that says, "You are a burden to me." Some of us find it difficult to be sensitive, but it is an attitude of heart that must be cultivated. Without sensitivity, the emotional baggage that our church members carry will get more acute rather than lessen. Churches should be havens where emotionally damaged people feel safe and have the confidence to deal with the issues that haunt them.

Look to God for healing

It is also vital that we recognise God's role in our pastoral care. The people to whom we minister were created by God in the first place, so he knows better than we what they need. In his omniscience, God knows exactly what circumstances have caused the damage and, surely, the remedy that will bring healing. I have often found myself in a situation where I really don't know what to do for the person I am trying to help, or even what to say to them. Human fallibility greatly limits our pastoral effectiveness. In such circumstances, prayer and listening to God is the only way forward. But when we do this we must believe that God can and will make a difference, and will bring healing to the wounded person that we are caring for. Faith is therefore a vital component in pastoral work. We should be quick to offer prayer and also committed to pray as the ultimate solution comes from God alone.

Beware of being swallowed by the monster of dependence

From a practical point of view, it is important to bear in mind that, although the church needs to care for people who are hurting, wisdom is also needed in deciding just what level of help to give and how it should be given. There are two potential problems that can result from handling emotional baggage. First, it is possible for church leaders to become so wrapped up in people's problems that they neglect their other duties. This can be a very real problem, because some people would absorb all of a leader's available time and still ask for more. Second, a person with emotional baggage could become so wrapped up in themselves that they begin to find security in their problems and do not want to move on and deal with them. What is more, their self-absorption will prevent them from being able to make any kind of contribution to the wider life of the church. Their problems must therefore be dealt with.

This does not mean that we should pull back on our compassion for hurting people. That should never be the case. But we do need to exercise wisdom, otherwise everyone ends up losing in the long run. In my church, we have tried to come up with a policy on pastoral care. We are willing to help anyone and spend as much time with them as is needed, provided they are willing to do something about their problems. While fully recognising that these could be long-term, we expect to see a measure of progress. In addition, we want to see at least a desire on the part of the people we are helping to be part of the church and to make a contribution. This contribution may well be small, but we want to see people giving and not just taking all the time. If these conditions are met, then we are more than happy to invest in their troubled lives. If not, then we will not commit very much time and energy to them. This may sound harsh, but it is a realistic necessity.

Discussion Questions

1. Evaluate how good your church is at dealing with people's baggage and why?
2. How can you develop a tolerance culture in your church without lowering standards?

CHAPTER 14
Final Reflection

My family loves the beach; sadly, however, the weather in Scotland means that we don't get to one very often. If the sun does shine, however, we head down to Ayr, where there is a beautiful beach and nice restaurants nearby where we can get something to eat. On rare occasions when my family allow me to choose where we will eat, I take them to a restaurant not far from the seafront where a good steak and a drink will not break the bank. This particular establishment is in what was an old church building, complete with high pointed roof and beautiful stone masonry. If we arrive in good time we are able to sit at an elevated table just below where the old pulpit was. I love the atmosphere of the place, but always feel a little sad to think that this building was once a place of worship but is now just a tavern with atmosphere.

These days this is not unusual. The UK is dotted with former church buildings that are now abandoned or bingo halls or trendy flats. These buildings were never meant to be used in this way, but with the decline of Christianity their original purpose is no longer relevant. The big question that now needs to be asked is whether or not further decline is inevitable. Jesus asked the question: "When the Son of Man returns, will he find faith on the earth? (Luke 18: 8). This is a question that every Christian must now ask.

Evangelicals can often be good at wringing their hands and lamenting the terrible world that we live in. This may be cathartic, but it is of little value. What is needed is real and assertive action. In 1914 Lord Kitchener was appointed as war minister to lead the battle against the Germans. His motto was a simple 'Britain needs you', and no one of that generation could have escaped the stern and challenging look of Kitchener's face and pointed finger on the thousands of posters dotted all over the country. But his call to mobilisation worked and some 3,000,000 joined the armed services.

The church today needs a similar clarion call. We are in the midst of the greatest battle of human history, one that has been waged continually in every corner of the earth since the Fall. It is the battle for the spiritual lives of men and women. God in his great mercy has brought about revivals all over the world. Indeed, the balance of the worldwide Church has changed, and now the great world centres of Christianity are places such as Africa, Latin America and Asia. Revival is well overdue in the United Kingdom today. Though revival is the sovereign work of God, as his Church we still have the obligation to reach out to a dying world with the message of hope and life through the death of Christ. This message is our world's only hope.

As I have tried to point out in this book, the problem is that the Church is all too often out of touch and remote from the community to which it is sent with the gospel. This must change if there is to be any hope for our friends, colleagues and neighbours who do not know Jesus Christ for themselves. We must act now!

Action, however, will only come about if Christians want to be busy in the work of evangelism. Sadly, my experience has been that many Christians are simply not motivated enough when it comes to the difficult business of sharing the gospel with others. All too many Christians let an opportunity pass, rather than speak up and say something that will make friends and colleagues think about their spiritual needs. Few take the trouble to create opportunities in which they will be able to say something. If this situation persists, then the days ahead will be dark for many churches in the United Kingdom. The situation is urgent and we must act now.

Discussion Questions

1. What are the biggest barriers to your church being successful in evangelism and how could you deal with them?
2. What can you do to encourage more people in your church to get involved with evangelism?

APPENDIX

Special Cases

So far in this book we have been looking at some of the broad principles involved in evangelism. However, there are specific segments of our society that deserve particular emphasis, because of the challenge of reaching them. This appendix section will deal with some of them. We will look at the particular challenge of reaching men and also people from other religious backgrounds. The first of these is important, because men are more hesitant than women to commit themselves to faith. The second is important because particular issues need to be thought about when it comes to reaching people from non-Christian religions. We will then look at reaching young people, not because they are particularly hard to reach, but because reaching them is strategic. Most of today's Christians in the UK became so when they were young.

Reaching men

When Jesus began his public ministry he chose twelve men to be his disciples. Many Bible scholars point out that there is significance in the number twelve, as this was also the number of tribes in the nation of Israel. I would also want to note that there is also significance in the fact that these disciples were all men. I am not suggesting that there was any sexism involved here; after all, there were women who followed Jesus too, and they were welcomed by him. The significant thing, however, was in the fact that for these men, following Jesus became such a natural thing. Some of them were colourful characters. There were impetuous and calloused-handed fishermen like Peter, aggressive and competitive men like James and John and even a terrorist, Simon the Zealot. For them there was nothing un-manly about worshipping Jesus, they were able to thrive in their faith, while at the same time enjoying their masculinity.

Given this background, it is perhaps surprising that so few men in our culture respond to the call of the gospel and become Christians. In many parts of the UK, churchgoing and Christianity are seen as appropriate for old people, women and children, but not for men. The statistics in many churches bear testimony to this attitude. In most churches there are fewer men than women, and in some congregations men occupy as little as 20% of the church roll.

There are a number of reasons why at least some churches do not appeal to men. First, much of Christian teaching appeals to the softer part of our natures. We are encouraged to be gentle and kind, to be forgiving and turn the other cheek. The Bible tells us that we are to love one another and to live humbly, putting the needs of others before our own. Arguably, these virtues are more appealing to women than to men. Often churches promote a genteel, cautious and compassionate lifestyle, and this is something that men often struggle with.

Then there is the issue which I refer to as 'homo-erotic' hymnology. Just imagine you are an alpha male and you have been invited to come to a church service. During the service, you are invited to sing about a man called Jesus, and you look at the screen at the front of the church and among the hymns there are the following lines:

- Jesus, lover of my soul, from you nothing I withhold
- Jesus, sweet Jesus, what a wonder you are
- May the fragrance of Jesus fill my life
- Jesus, your name is like honey on my lips
- Oh Lord you're beautiful, your face is all I seek
- Draw me close to you, never let me go
- I'm desperate for you, I'm lost without you
- Let my words be few, Jesus I'm so in love with you

How comfortable would you or the average man feel as he sings these words? If hymns are a little embarrassing, what about church activities? You decide you will become a Christian and get involved in the life of the church, but what will you actually do? In the average church, the options for service would include crèche, junior church, catering team, welcome team, home visitation and the after-schools club. All of these are valid ministries; however, few would be appealing to the average man.

Given the issues above, how do we begin to reach men, and make the gospel and church attractive to them? This is a huge issue, and whole books have been written on the subject. It is impossible to say very much, given the limitations of space, but there are a few things that need to be mentioned which might shed a little light. First, we need to create or develop positive role models in the life of the church. We need Christian men to be real men and to boldly marry their faith with their masculinity. Nothing will be more impressive to other men than a man who is a real leader, a real man's man, who at the same time is very open about his commitment to Jesus. His honest straight talking will in itself give 'permission' for other men to listen and follow.

Second, churches need to have events that are specifically attractive to men. Often this will involve having an active sports programme in the church, as this is something that interests many men. However, there are social events that can also be geared specifically to men, such as quiz nights, movie clubs, motorbike rides, fishing and camping trips, lads and their dads events or even events which appeal to the intellect, such as debating groups.

Third, it is important to build a sense of companionship among men already in the church, but one that welcomes outsiders. Men need a sense of belonging. They need peers who they can talk to frankly and openly and also laugh with. This is true whether they are Christians or not. The gospel can readily be communicated in a context where a group of men, Christian and non-Christian, enjoy each other's company and spend quality time together.

Fourth, it is important to emphasize the significance of the role that men play in life, and to demonstrate that the gospel can impact these roles. For example, many men are both husbands and fathers. In reality, a significant proportion of men do not play these roles well. Our whole society is damaged by unfaithful husbands and absentee fathers. The essential dignity of being a husband and a father should be taught as part of our gospel proclamation. We should also stress that, in these very practical areas, the gospel can transform, as God's power enables us to be the men that we ought to be. This can be backed up practically by events based on teaching these roles.

Reaching men will never be easy. However, if a little thought is given to how we reach out and what we say when given the opportunity, we are more likely to make more of an impact.

Reaching people of other faiths[1]

The past few decades have witnessed a greater ethnic diversity all over Europe and certainly in the UK. While immigration is an important political issue at the moment, things are not likely to change, as our low birth rate, shortage of skills, porous borders and the continuing influence of globalisation will make further immigration inevitable. Whatever we may think of this situation, it certainly presents an exciting opportunity for gospel proclamation. We live now in a country with two million Muslims, 600,000 Hindus, 400,000 Sikhs, 250,000 Jews, 212,000 Buddhists and 220,000 people from other non-Christian religions. At least some of these people, if they still lived in their country of origin, would be very hard to reach with the gospel.

While we have freedom of religion in the UK, and also freedom to pro-claim our faith, the challenge of reaching people from other world religions is still a major one. Even before we begin to think about how to communicate the gospel effectively, we need to get a proper perspective about what we are dealing with. This is particularly the case when it comes to witnessing to Muslims within our culture. The popular press has a tendency to demonise Muslims, as if they were all mindless and dangerous extremists. Islam, of course, does pose a significant threat to world peace, and there are many extremists throughout the globe as well as in the UK. Furthermore, there is room within Islamic theology to allow for violent behaviour. That said, the majority of Muslims in the UK will not be extreme: they are law abiding citizens who are well integrated into this culture and are concerned about the issue of extremism also. Many Muslims who live in the UK and the West

---

1   Written with help from Derek Malcolm, director of Firm Foundations

in general do so because they want to escape from the tyranny of the Islamic states they have come from, and they find the freedoms in the West something that they greatly value. Unless we see them in this way, and build real relationships with them, we are unlikely to be successful in reaching them.

Not only do we need to get a proper perspective on what we are dealing with, we also need correct thinking about non-Christian religions. This is important, because how we think about other religions will largely determine how we do evangelism with people who believe in them. Historically, there has been a spectrum of belief among Christians about the issue. Some Christians have had a completely negative view of all non-Christian religions and have seen them as utterly false in every way, and even demonic. Others have had a much more sympathetic view of other religions, and have admired the sincerity with which many Muslim, Hindu and Buddhist believers hold to their faith. Some Christians have even gone as far as to claim that, while Jesus is the perfect way to God, there are nevertheless lesser pathways which, while not the ideal, will still bring the worshipper favour with God. This more radical perspective has led to a kind of universalism in which, it is claimed, sincere believers will get into heaven by following their religion, even if they don't have a personal faith in Christ.

The issue is, of course, complex, but it is important to think about what the Bible actually says. When we look at the Gospels, as they tell the story of the birth of Jesus, we see something very interesting. Among those who came to see the baby Jesus and to worship him were a group of wise men, or magi. These were probably Persian mystics who had some kind of contact with Judaism as a result of the Babylonian exile. They were not Jews, and part of their source of revelation was through reading the stars. This may seem a spurious way of hearing truth, yet they grasped that someone of significance was born, and they travelled many miles to come and worship. This interesting and strange story should be read in conjunction with Acts 4: 12, where we read that salvation is found in no one else than Jesus, for there is no other name under heaven given to mankind by which we must be saved. Clearly, Jesus is the way of salvation and no other religion can offer any hope, salvation or merit before God. Yet it does seem from the birth narratives that God in his grace is able to communicate through general revelation, and this might include aspects of the belief system of other world religions. That is not to say that these religions are correct, they are not! However, there might be some light in what they believe, and this can be a connection point with them that can be used as inroads for evangelism. For example, when I witness to Muslims, it certainly helps the situation that they believe in one God who reveals himself, they believe in sin and punishment and they believe in the historic person of Jesus Christ. We do, of course, need to be a little cautious here, because the Islamic concept of God and sin is different from the Christian concept, and Jesus is only seen as the second to last prophet. Nevertheless, conversations on these subjects are a good starting-point, and one that we need to make use of.

We should also note that many people from other religions share some of our values, such as a concern for where an increasingly secular UK society is going, the disintegration of families, the wanton pursuit of materialism, the moving away from and ridiculing of faith in general. These concerns are easy for us to identify with, and they also provide a natural point of conversation and a means for building understanding and a relationship with them.

When it comes to witnessing to people from other faiths, there are a number of basic things that we must remember in our approach. Firstly, we need to show genuine respect for the person. Many of the people we witness to will come from a different cultural perspective and sense of identity. Unless we show that we value them as people in their own right, it will be hard to develop the kind of relationship that makes genuine dialogue possible. Part of this respect must surely be a willingness to defend religious liberty for all. Some Christians are very concerned about preserving liberty for Christians, but less enthusiastic about liberty for others. Again this attitude is the wrong basis for a genuine relationship.

Second, it is also important that we admit to the weaknesses of Christendom. There have been many things done in the name of Christianity that are an affront to true Christians. The Crusades, the Apartheid regime and the Spanish Inquisition, to name just a few. While it is certainly true that Jesus himself would have been deeply opposed to all of these things, yet those who perpetrated these evils bore his name and we cannot escape from this. It should also be pointed out that Christendom is not alone in perpetrating abuses. Muslims participated in the slave trade, the Armenian genocide, the persecution of Sikhs, and many terrible wars. This does not excuse the sins of Christendom, but does contribute to a balanced reading of history. We need to openly tell those we witness to that these deeds were evil and that no true Christian could ever sanction them. Coupled with this honesty, there must be a respect for the other person's religion and commitment. This does not mean we agree with what they believe—we don't. But insulting and belittling another person's faith position is never good.

Most of all, we just need to show the love of Christ. I once saw a public debate between a Christian and a Muslim in which it was obvious that the arguments the Christian was using were much more powerful than those of his opponents. What was more impressive, however, was the manner of the debate. The Christian was warm and friendly, as well as very courteous. He went out of his way to build a relationship, even during the debate itself. Afterwards, the brother of the Muslim was being interviewed and interestingly he made the comment that the Christian showed real love for his brother. This attitude is precisely the one we need as we share the gospel with people.

Having thought about the approach we must make, we now need to think about the content of our proclamation. One defining verse that we need to think about is John 14: 6, where Jesus said, 'I am the way, the truth and the life, no one comes to the Father but by me'. This was unambiguous, laying down a direct challenge to people of all religions to follow Christ. Without him, there is no access to God and no salvation. If this is the case, then in our evangelism with people of other faiths we need to keep talking about Jesus and the evidence that he is the Son of God. If we elevate Christ, we will reach others (John 12: 32).

As we go around talking about Jesus to our friends from other world religions, there are some things we need to remember. First, actions speak louder than words. It matters little what we say, if they cannot see Christ in our lives. Second, patience is a virtue. If a person has spent their whole life steeped in a very different religion, they are unlikely to change as a result of a quick conversation. It might take dozens, if not hundreds, of conversations over many months and years. Third, it is always important to remember the common ground you share, and use that to open conversations. Fourth, remember that culture plays a huge role, and someone who is a Muslim, for example, will have a whole cultural outlook and lifestyle wrapped up in their belief system. This must be taken into consideration as you witness. Fifth, be aware of important non-verbal cues. If a Muslim comes into you home and you are eating pork and drinking alcohol, this will immediately be a stumbling block. If you set your Bible on the floor or put something else on top of it, that will communicate to him something negative about your attitude to God's word. Sixth, always remember that love will always be the key.

If you have contact with people from other religious backgrounds, it is important to get good resources that will enable you to understand their faith and also how to witness to them. Just be aware that too little knowledge can be a dangerous thing, because it leads to inaccurate assumptions. For example, some Christians think that all Muslims are basically the same. Actually nothing could be further from the truth. Within Islam, there are not only the two major branches of Sunni and Shia, there are also lots of sects and people groups who differ greatly, but still call themselves Muslim. We need to really understand who we are talking to, so that we communicate accurately and meaningfully.

Reaching the non-religious

Some missiologists believe that the three great forces that will dominate the world over the next century will be Christianity, Islam and militant atheism. Certainly, within the UK, we see each of these forces at work, and arguably the most potent within our culture is atheism. In a world where religion plays a key role, it in alarming to see how vigorous and confident atheism has become within European and British culture. We should not see it merely as a Western phenomenon either, as a recent report claimed that over 1 billion of the world's population claimed no religious belief at all.[2]

It is important, as we begin to think about this issue, that we get our definitions correct, because non-religious people vary greatly across a wide spectrum. On one side, there are the evangelistic and militant atheists like Richard Dawkins, and on the other, there are the people who simply do not

---

2   http://www.dailymail.co.uk/news/article-2250096/You-wouldnt-believe-atheism-worlds-biggest-faith-Christianity-Islam.html

go to any place of worship. They are very different, and motivated in different ways, but all under the broad category of non-religious.

When we come to look at definitions, we begin with atheism, which is the commitment to a belief that God does not exist. In that sense, atheists are on the hard edge of non-religion. It is not just that they have doubts, it is more than that: they are committed to the belief that there is no God. Even here, there is a spectrum as far as attitude goes. Some atheists are that because they think there is little evidence for God, but it is a gentle philosophical commitment. They are not against religious people, they just think them to be wrong. Nevertheless, they can have a respect for religious positions and even see some value in religion. A good example of this is the journalist Matthew Parris, an atheist who thinks Christianity is a great force for good in Africa (John Lennox, *Gunning for God*, p.78). Some atheists however are militant in their belief and want to convert the whole world to their atheist agenda. They are impassioned, in part, because they believe that religion is an evil in the world and therefore needs to be fought against. Good examples of this are Richard Dawkins and the late Christopher Hitchins.

Then we think about agnostics, who are often honest seekers who are simply not sure what to believe. They would not hold to the dogmatism of atheism and would not declare with confidence that there is no God. Rather, they would say that God is unknowable, or that there is not enough evidence to decide one way or the other that God exists.

Finally there are people who could simply be described as 'secular'. They are not specifically committed to a philosophical position, such as atheism or agnosticism; they simply do not value religious faith and inhabit a world where religion has no place.

When we come to think of witnessing to non-religious people, there are three challenges that we might need to be prepared for. First, many non-religious people make the assumption that they occupy the intellectual high ground. This is because many claim that their worldview is based on science and empirical evidence, unlike religious people whose worldview is based on faith. This leads us to a second and related challenge. Whenever we engage in dialogue with people who are non-religious, they will often make the assumption that they are speaking and thinking in a very different realm from us. Their realm is that of science, logic, fact and truth. They would see the religious realm as that of faith, assumption and subjectivity.

A third challenge will be what evidence and explanations can be accepted as valid. Many non-religious people, especially atheists, will subscribe consciously or unconsciously to philosophical naturalism, that is, the belief that all that exists is the physical, material (natural) world. This is a very reductionist and limited perspective, but one that can cause problems in our witnessing. Some years ago, I was talking to a young atheist who believed that science provides ultimate answers to life's questions. He was convinced of the theory of evolution, and we spent some time discussing it together. I raised some important objections to evolution which he struggled to answer, but nevertheless replied that even if he could not prove that evolution was true, something like it must be the case because there needed to be a material explanation for life. This was a clear declaration of naturalism. He was not open to any explanation for life that was outside of the natural world.

How do we begin to witness to non-religious people? What needs to be said to penetrate their scepticism? The first thing that we need to do is to debunk the myth that there is some inherent conflict between belief in God and science. The very fact the some of the great fathers of science (Newton, Kepler, Faraday) and leading scientists today also believe in God (Lennox, Collins, Heap, Meyer) suggests there is no intrinsic conflict. There is a sense in which science provides an explanation for mechanism based on observation, though it does not give us a cause. Faith deals with the cause issue.

Having made that point, we also have to deal with science properly. Christians have often been guilty of deprecating science, and also creating a false conflict between faith and science. For example, some Christians assume that if any aspect of the theory of evolution were to be accepted, then we are automatically unfaithful to Scripture. This is patently false. The Genesis narratives are a product of the pre-scientific age and there are dangers in trying to read science into Moses' words. Creating this conflict obscures us from the facts, blurs the argument and prevents us from getting to the real issue. Indeed, in practice I tend to avoid talking about evolution, except to point out that it does not provide an explanation for cause, and as a theory it has significant weaknesses. However, I do not take too much time to disprove it (which is very hard to do), and I emphasize my belief in a creator God, who intricately designed this universe and continues to maintain it. What I do not do is ridicule science and scientists. Indeed, like Newton, I believe in the importance of science precisely because behind the orderly and rationally intelligible universe there is a creator.

The next thing we need to do is to challenge them to follow the evidence wherever it leads. This includes not only scientific evidence but evidence from history, philosophy and human intuition. This actually is a strongpoint for us. As Paul reminded us, creation itself bears the hallmarks of evidence for God (Rom. 1:20). If we want to deal with the evidence honestly, there is much to be found and this must be driven home. We need to particularly focus on the historical Jesus. This evidence is not only deeply compelling, it leads us to the essence of the Christian message.

The final thing that needs to be done is that we need to live it out, because our own lives are the most powerful message that we can preach. This is because, when it comes to the really big issues in life such as sickness, tragedy, justice and death, atheism has nothing to say. By contrast, I had a Christian friend with great abilities and intellect who contracted MS at a relatively young age. She lived much of her life in a wheelchair before becoming bedridden, and then finally she died. However, throughout her life she had hope, joy, and a sense of her own self-worth, a true perspective in life, and upon death she was released from her broken body into an eternal life in Paradise. In the face of this kind of experience, the non-religious offer only cold and empty despair.

Reaching young people[3]

If you were to do a survey in an average evangelical church and ask the church members when they became Christians, the majority would state it was when they were young. Probably they were under fifteen years of age, and had some involvement in the life of the church through a youth club, a children's club or a relationship with someone in the church. It is for this reason that we need to think about reaching young people for Christ. They are not the most difficult

---

3 Written with help from Allison Hill, GLO administrator and schools worker.

group of people within our society to reach, in fact there is a real openness to the spiritual realm. Arguably, however, they are the most important, given the sheer numbers of people who become Christians at this stage in life, and because the cynicism of adulthood has not yet begun.

Life has changed significantly for young people over the past few decades, and any evangelism strategy must take this change into account. While there are many loving and stable families, giving coherence to the very fabric of society, there are also families that are highly dysfunctional. There are now more single-parent families, latch-key kids, absentee fathers and delinquent children than there have been for generations. It would be wrong to think that every young person who comes into the orbit of your church has social challenges, but many will, and we need to be prepared for this.

As we think about reaching young people, we need to remember the world they inhabit. Today's generation of children enter a world that is troubled, and because of the media saturation, it is a world they know a great deal about. They view the world through an idealistic lens; but as they are getting 'older' younger, they are much less naive that we often suppose. Innocence is lost, and the confusion and hypocrisy that dominates our society is not hidden from them, even though they do not always have the emotional apparatus to appropriately deal with what they know and see. Their lives are influenced by peer pressure, popular culture, and the mass media, and they function daily within a highly sexualised and techno-centric society. As they get older, the role of the adult diminishes, as they increase in confidence, sophistication and independence.

When it comes to reaching young people with the gospel, the key issue is relationship. Churches can often fall into the trap of assuming that a flashy multi-media programme is what will attract young people to faith. While presentation is important, it is much less significant than the love that we can show young people. If they want to be entertained, they will go to the cinema; church needs to be the place of quality and dependable relationships, and, if this is provided, they will recognise its value. We should also bear in mind that many young people do not enjoy positive and meaningful relationships with adults, especially if their family background leaves much to be desired. In this way every church member has a role to play in being a spiritual uncle, aunt, grandmother or even parent. While age-appropriate programmes, such and 'junior church', are valuable, they have the unintended consequences of keeping the generations apart. It is important, for these reasons, that children are part of the church community, so that they can have input from everyone and feel a sense of belonging - not to a 'children's event', but to the church. As churches, we need to consider intergenerational ministry, because young people instinctively know the value of family and can identify it in church life.

If church is to be this positive experience for young people, there are some things that we must avoid. First, we need to ensure that we take them seriously. Children mattered in Scripture, and truly biblical Christianity needs to acknowledge this. Children are to be seen and heard, and if church members belittle or marginalise children, or even give the impression that they are an inconvenience, then they will not stay. We need to remember that when Jesus told the parable of the lost sheep (Mt. 18: 10), he was referring to children. Every one of them is to be sought out, and we should not give up until they are included.

Second, we need to be role-models of the faith. Children learn through observation and experience and have a high expectation of adults. If how we live is different from what we say, worse still, if how we live is different from what we tell children they should be like, then the damage can be immense. There is nothing worse than a Christian in church who is grumpy, selfish, complaining, arrogant or intolerant. How can we expect children to become like Jesus, if the adults who are meant to be examples are not? Churches should never expect the children to rise above the spiritual level of the adults. It is particularly important that men 'role-model' the Christian life, as children often live their lives surrounded by women and they do not make a connection between masculinity and church.

Third, we must never patronise children. They have a positive contribution to make to the church community, and any church full of children will also be full of life, colour, noise and laughter. They hate being talked down to by adults. Equally they hate being squeezed into a mould, made to feel they only fit in if they behave like adults, and not being allowed to be themselves. We also need to acknowledge that their frank approach, their lack of political correctness, and their uncluttered perspective, can speak powerfully into the life of the church. Why can't children be a prophetic voice in the church?

As we look to the future, we need to bear in mind that children are the church of today and not just the church of the future. We need to invest heavily in them with our time, money, energy and emotions. It is important not just to pray for children but to pray with them, and to show them what a dynamic relationship with Christ looks like. Allow children to be children, and do not confuse adolescent behaviour with a lack of spirituality. Have the flexibility to make church a meaningful and rewarding experience for children. It is no coincidence that the New Testament describes church as a family. Sadly, we have often turned it into a business, a school, a social club or even a retirement home. It needs to be a family where everyone has a sense of belonging, whatever their age, and where everyone engages with each other. If church is a place where we expect everyone to learn and grow, then this vision will impact adults and children alike.

For Further Reading

Useful Books on Apologetics

by William Lane Craig
Apologetics An Introduction (Moody)
No Easy Answers (Moody)
Reasonable Faith (Crossways)

by Ravi Zacharias
Can Man Live without God? (Word)
Jesus Among other Gods (Word)

by John Lennox
God's Undertaker: has science buried God? (Lion)
Gunning for God: why the New Atheists are missing the target (Lion)

Darwin on Trial by Philip Johnson (Monarch)
Know Why you Believe by Paul Little (IVP)
If God, Then What? by Andrew Wilson (IVP)
Scaling the Secular City by J.P. Moreland (Baker)
Christian Apologetics by Douglas Groothuis (Apollos)

Useful Books on Culture and Postmodernity

A Primer on Postmodernism by Stanley Grenz (Eerdmans)

Evangelicals and Truth by Peter Hicks (IVP)

The Gagging of God by Don Carson (Zondervan)

Truth Decay by Douglas Groothuis (IVP)

Postmodern Times by Gene Veith (Crossways)

Useful books on Other Religions and Religious Pluralism

Dissonant Voices by Harold A Netland (Apollos)

A Christian's Evangelistic Pocket Guide to Islam by Malcolm Steer (Christian Focus)

The Challenge of Islam to the Church and its Mission, by Patrick Sookhdeo (Isaac Publishing)

Useful Books on Evangelism, Church Planting and Church Growth

Everyday Church by Tim Chester (IVP)

Fresh Shoots on Stony Ground edited by Stephen McQuoid and Neil Summerton (Partnership/CPI)

The Purpose Driven Church by Rick Warren (Zondervan)

Evangelism through the Local Church by Michael Green (Hodder & Stoughton)

Why Men Hate Going to Church by David Murrow (Nelson)

Bibliography

BEBBINGTON, D.W., *Evangelicalism in Modern Britain*, Routledge, 1989

BRIERELY, Peter, UK Christian Handbook 2000/2001, *Religious Trends*, No.2, Harper Collins

BROWN, Colin, *Christianity & Western Thought* Vol.1, Apollos, 1990

BRUCE, F.F., *The Book of Acts*, New London Commentary, Marshall Morgan & Scott, 1968

CANE, Herbert, *The Christian World Mission: Today and Tomorrow*, Baker, 1981

CARSON, Don, *The Gagging of God*, Zondervan, 1996

CARSON, Don, *The Gospel According to John*, IVP, 1991

CHEESMAN, Graham, *Hyperchoice*, IVP, 1998

CHESTER, Tim & TIMMIS, Steve, , *Everyday Church*, IVP, 2011

COLLINSON, Diane, *Fifty Major Philosophers*, Routledge, 1997

COPLEY, Terence, *About the Bible*, Bible Society, 1990

CRAGIE, Peter, *Psalms 1-50*, WBC vol.19, Word, 1986

CRAIG, William L, *Apologetics An Introduction*, Moody Press, 1984

CRAIG, William L, *No Easy Answers*, Moody Press, 1990

CRAIG, William L, *Reasonable Faith*, Crossway Books, 1994

DEMBSKI, William Ed., *Mere Creation*, IVP, 1998

DRANE, John, *Cultural Change and Biblical Faith*, Paternoster, 2000

EDEN, Martyn Ed., *Britain on the Brink*, Crossway Books, 1990

ERICKSON, Millard, *Christian Theology*, Baker Books, 1998

GAY, Craig, *The Way of the Modern World*, Eerdmans, 1998

GILL, David & GEMPF, C. Eds, *The Book of Acts in its First Century Setting*, Vol.2, Eerdmans, 1994

GRENZ, Stanley, *A Primer on Postmodernism*, Eerdmans, 1996

GROOTHUIS, Douglas, *Truth Decay*, IVP, 2000

HALL, D.R., *Illustrated Bible Dictionary*, IVP, 1980

JOHNSTONE, Patrick, *Operation World*, OM Publishing, 2010

JOHNSTON, Phillip, *Darwin on Trial*, Monarch, 1991

JOSEPHUS, *The Complete Works of Josephus*, Kregel, 1981

KORAN, *The Koran*, Penguin Books, 1990 edition

LARKIN, William, *Acts*, New Testament Commentary, IVP, 1995

LENNOX, John, *God's Undertaker: has Science Buried God*, Lion, 2009

LENNOX, John, *Gunning for God: why the New Atheists and Missing the Target*, Lion 2011

LEUPOLD, H.C., *Exposition of Psalms*, Baker, 1990

LEWIS, C.S., *God in the Dock*, Collins, 1979

LITTLE, Paul, *Know Why You Believe*, IVP, 2000

LONGENECKER, Richard, *Acts*, Expositor's Bible Commentary, Zondervan, 1995

MARCH, Ruth, *Europe Reborn*, OM Publishing, 1992

MARSHALL, Howard, *Acts*, TNTC, IVP, 1980

MCDOWELL, Josh, *The Resurrection Factor*, Here's Life Publishers, 1981

MCQUOID, Stephen, *A Guide to God's Family*, Paternoster Press, 2000

MCQUOID, Stephen, *A New Kind of Living*, Christian Focus Publications, 1998

MICHAELS, Ramsey, *1 Peter*, Word Biblical Commentary, Word, 1988

MOO, Douglas, *The Epistle to the Romans*, Eerdmans, 1996

MURRAY, Stuart, *Church Planting*, Paternoster Press, 1998

NELSON, David, *Why Men Hate Going to Church,* Thomas Nelson, 2005

NETLAND, Harold, *Dissonant Voices: Religious Pluralism and the Question of Truth,* Apollos, 1991

NORTON, Mark, Texts and Manuscripts of the Old Testament, Ed. PW Comfort, *The Origin of the Bible*, Tyndale, 1992

PALEY, William, *Natural Theology*, Ed. John Hick, The Existence of God, Macmillan, 1964

REAPER, William and SMITH, Linda, *A Brief Guide to Ideas*, Lion, 1997

RUSSELL, Bertrand, *History of Western Philosophy*, Routledge, 1991

SINE, Tom, *Mustard Seed versus McWorld*, Monarch, 1999

STARK, Rodney, *The Triumph of Christianity*, Harper One, 2011

STOLL, David, *Is Latin America Turning Protestant?* University of California Press, 1990

STOTT, John, *The Message of Acts*, BST, IVP, 1990

TOFFLER, Alvin, *Future Shock*, Pan Books, 1973

SOOKHDEO, Patrick, *The Challenge of Islam to the Church and its Mission*, Isaac Publishing, 2009

VEITH, Gene, *Guide to Contemporary Culture*, Crossway Books, 1994

WANAMAKER, Charles, *The Epistle to the Thessalonians*, Commentary on the Greek Text, Eerdmans, 1990

WILLIAMS, Peter, *The Case for God*, Monarch, 1999

WILSON, Andrew, *If God then What?*, IVP, 2012

ZACHARIAS, Ravi, *Jesus among other Gods*, Word Books, 2000

ZACHARIAS, Ravi, *Can Man Live without God*, Word Books, 1994